MYSTIC RHYTHMS

MYSTIC RHYTHMS:

The Philosophical Vision of RUSH

Carol Selby Price & Robert M. Price

WILDSIDE PRESS
BERKELEY HEIGHTS, NJ • 1999

MYSTIC VISIONS

Published by:

Wildside Press
P.O. Box 45
Gillette, NJ 07933-0045
www.wildsidepress.com

INTRODUCTION

"I respect her judgment, you know, though she's doing a think piece on a rock star..."

—Woody Allen, *Manhattan*

What can be redeemed of the Seventies? It is a decade most of us seem to remember with a wince as a time of joltingly bad dress, kitsch, and Disco music. As a decade it stood in the shadow of the mind-expanding Sixties. The Seventies seemed caught in a collective failure of nerve after its big brother decade. The cultural radicals of the Sixties did their work too well, it seemed. Many of their manners and mores succeeded in making it into the mainstream, but they were diluted in the process.

Student demonstrators finally convinced enough of their elders that the Vietnam War was just more trouble than it could possibly be worth, so the troops came home. But the long-range result was a paralysis when it came to matters of international crises. We as a country wanted no part of anything that stood half a chance of becoming another Vietnam. The decade ended in national despair over the Iranian hostage crisis. We could not persuade ourselves to use force—or not to. It was the depth of President Jimmy Carter's "malaise," of the Seventies themselves.

The sexual revolution took hold everywhere. The churches began rethinking their moral prescriptions—to the outrage of hidebound traditionalists and to the apathy of everyone else, who proceeded quietly to do what felt right, unhampered by Victorian morality. Pot became a party drug for many of those who had previously damned it, even as they sipped another highball.

Dress styles were commercialized. "Radical" became what Tom Wolfe called "radical chic." But only to a point. It was pure style, pure pose, and thus no one wanted to go too far. The Seventies with their sideburns and garish kitchen colors and drippy guitar-and-muted-trumpet music, were really sort of a network TV version of the Sixties: denatured, caricatured, timid shadows of the real thing.

Is there anything in this tepid, commercialized decade to save, or to savor? This has become an urgent question for many of us in "Generation X"—the generation that grew up seeing Sixties sitcoms in syndication and the first run of *The Brady Bunch*. The popular culture

5

that seems to have so defined the "thirty-somethings" already seemed stale to us, though we may have had subliminal memories of some of those Sixties albums heard in the womb or the crib. But our own pop culture seemed stale, too! *Father Knows Best* seems pretty lame now, true, but *The Brady Bunch* was just a poor Xerox of it! "Talkin' about my generation"—sad but true.

I think there is one exception to the rule of pop-cultural decay in the inglorious decade of the Seventies. There was one respect in which the Seventies witnessed the ripening of the Sixties. I am thinking of FM Rock (*i.e.*, Hard, Classical, and/or Art Rock). I have in mind and memory (and on Compact Disc) the music of a handful of groups, including Genesis, Yes, Jethro Tull, Led Zeppelin, King Crimson, Pink Floyd, Renaissance—and Rush. These were the days, yes, the despised Seventies, when Rock reached its peak.

I was a teenager then, living to no apparent purpose in one of the bedroom communities Rush sings about in "Subdivisions," congregating with my indifferent peers in basement bars and shopping malls. Our lives were simply part of the scenery of the weekend existence of our parents, who had created suburban lives as places to go when they weren't busy at the office.

Sometimes such parents just can't seem to see that they have created a world that their kids need to escape from just as much as they themselves needed to escape from their work and come home to relax. One person's Xanadu is another's prison. And for many teenagers, the main path of relief and escape is Rock.

Nothing has so defined the youth culture (or subculture) like Rock music. There are different kinds of Rock, and each kind attracts its devotees. Each style, with its principal groups, becomes a tribal totem. For me, the totem was FM Rock, the gods the groups I have listed. There was something about them that has since faded from the music scene, even from the later work of some of the same groups. Rush explains why in "The Spirit of Radio": artistic integrity selling out to mass market mediocrity.

Where are you going to find another Jethro Tull? Who else is going to even want to try a modern electric version of the authentic strains of old Celtic folk melodies that haunt the listener with the *frisson* of what seem for the moment ancestral memories of a greener, more heroic age?

Or think of Pink Floyd's lyrical world-weariness, its Proustian "remembrance of things past," its Dickensian plaints of a dungeon-like youth ("We don't need no education"), its awareness that life is one big irony, that the only perspective from which to understand it is the dark side of the moon, where one sees the obvious but otherwise unseen—you can't listen to this stuff without being forced to muse and reflect.

I rejoiced to retire for a moment from the suburban "life in two dimensions" to stand exposed to the soul-shaking sounds of the Mellatron in the Court of the Crimson King. Listening to Yes at their best was like letting the music weave a mood-map, launch a light-ship into new galaxies of meaning and motive.

You sometimes hear Rock criticized as the anthem of a new generation of low-brow hedonists, "feel-good" music for people with no aspiration higher than satisfying their basest instincts. "Sex, Drugs, Rock-&-Roll!" But that's just not the way it was with FM Rock. This was art.

These groups and their music formed the audio backdrop of my most formative years and experiences. I was the typical Rock fan, hanging with the "wrong crowd," the kids with no grades, who smoked dope and drank, and would occasionally get in trouble with the law, and then brag about it. Nothing like today's *Lord of the Flies*-style youth, mind you, but giving their parents genuine reason to be worried nonetheless.

I was, I say, pretty much the typical Rock fan—but, then again, I wasn't a fan of typical Rock. This is where what you listened to, what I listened to anyway, made all the difference. I listened to all the groups I have mentioned, but most of all I listened to Rush—Geddy Lee, Alex Lifeson, and Neil Peart—and I heard there what I heard in few other groups.

Today's Heavy Metal groups, whose music so alarms parents and church groups, sometimes defend themselves by pointing out that no one can hear most of what they're singing over the din anyway! I like the way horror writer T. E. D. Klein put it in his story, "Nadelman's God": "AC/DC, Iron Maiden, Twisted Sister, and a host of lesser-known bands...specialized in purveying a kind of loud, satanic rock that appealed mainly to prepubescent boys."

Another defense of these groups is that they're just kidding. They don't really believe, or mean anybody else ought to believe, all this stuff about suicide and Satanism. It's all an act, no more to be taken seriously than the ludicrous leering, posturing, and prancing across the stage in what was once called "fashionable pessimism."

You have no doubt read real-life horror stories about teenage listeners who unfortunately *have* taken these lyrics seriously. Murder, suicide, and even human sacrifice have been the occasional result. But the only danger I was in when as a teenager I hunkered down to read and reread Rush's lyrics (the ones I didn't know by heart already from hearing them countless times) was the "danger" of catching the contagion of the group's infectious optimism. I took it seriously when they sang about clues to some real motivation, dragging your dream into existence.

Listening, I became convinced that there was a future out there for me. That I needn't become another gum-snapping, pot-smoking clerk or checker looking back to High School as the zenith of my existence. As nostalgic as my story here may sound, I look back and value my youth listening to Rush precisely as the beginning of something better, a *future*. That's where I live now.

I picked up emotions and impressions from my Rush albums. But I also picked up what I didn't find at all in most groups: ideas. These are what most often get lost in the clamor of hopping hormones in the teenage years. But here, carried by Rock rhythms and electric riffs that ranked with the best the industry could offer, were ideas whose voices would not be shouted down.

Here, amid the vast wasteland of titanic sound lending cosmic grandeur and epic scope to insipid crises of puppy love and pimples, was a group propounding titanic thoughts with pounding rhythm to match. I owe it to Rush that ideas became a habit of life for me, and that I eventually followed where they led, pulling myself together for college-prep work. I was attracted to philosophy, and, seeing what it was doing for me, I began to dream of one day starting a program for teaching philosophy and critical thinking to young people like myself. Why shouldn't Thinking be an item on the educational agenda just as much as Math or English?

Imagine my surprise at discovering that my college, chosen for other reasons, also offered a graduate program in something called Philosophy for Children. After getting my B.A. in philosophy, I entered the Institute for the Advancement of Philosophy for Children.

And in the years since, my conviction that young people need the kind of guidance Rush offered me has only become stronger. You see, what Rush had done was to teach *me* philosophy. They didn't *call* it that, but that's what it *was*, and that's what they were doing. It was only several years later that I knew enough to start recognizing the sources of many of their ideas and principles and to start being able to put names to them.

If Rush was head and shoulders above most other groups in the Seventies, they remain so in the Nineties, having continued their work through all the intervening years. It is a testimony to Rush and the other vanguard groups of the Seventies that they still manage to hold an old audience and to draw to themselves new ones.

Once, during the course of writing this book, I formed a group of neighborhood teenagers to discuss Rush's lyrics. In listening to these young people, some of them musicians themselves, I was surprised and yet somehow not surprised at all to discover just who it was they were listening to. It seems they had gravitated not to the pop icons of their generation, but rather to most of the same artists who had fueled my youthful imagination!

Thus, I am convinced not only that today's generation needs to hear what Rush has to say, but that in very great numbers (as their sales and concert attendance figures both attest) they are in fact hearing it. The results can only be good.

It is my hope in the present volume to amplify the already loud reverberations of Rush's ideas a bit more. I want to make explicit some things left implicit in their songs. I want to explain some of the references the casual listener might not understand. As I see it, the songs try to awaken a curiosity in the listener. There are plenty of teasing phrases here and there which, like a half-forgotten dream, seem to hold much meaning, though we cannot quite crack the code. But I venture to claim that in several cases I have cracked it, or made a beginning, and I want to compare notes with the reader.

What I have done is to select several major songs by Rush's lyricist Neil Peart, and to organize my analyses of them according to theme. This was not hard to do. The songs lend themselves to such treatment quite naturally. I ignore the chronological order of writing or recording of the songs except where it is worth calling attention to some development of Rush's thought on a given subject.

I then take the songs one by one, concentrating on what I take to be the meaning of the lyrics. I explain some sections line by line; other, less esoteric ones, I discuss in more general terms. So I am trying to provide the thinking Rush listener with both a commentary on some of the more important songs and an exposition of the group's philosophical vision as a whole. It is organized into seven major themes, with a chapter devoted to each one.

If there are moments in their music when you have found yourself puzzled by what you hear, I hope this book will help you toward a better grasp of their lyrics. But I strongly suspect that most readers will experience frequent moments of recognition, deepening of an understanding they already have, as I did, from simply listening to the songs.

I am aware that a song is like a joke: if you have to explain it before someone gets it, it hasn't done its job well. I don't think that in that sense the songs require any explanation. I think they do their job quite well. But as I have said, part of the job they mean to do is to whet the appetite of the listener, to motivate him to dig deeper, to travel farther along the road on which the song has set his feet. And these chapters should help you go farther along that path. The books ends with a list of suggestions for further reading on the themes discussed in the chapters (and in the songs).

One word of warning. I cannot guarantee that in every case I have accurately mirrored what Neil Peart meant by a particular line or phrase. I am sure I use examples or illustrations that might not ever occur to him. I am, in other words, giving you my personal interpretation of his lyrics and of what I perceive to be his ideas. I am carrying them forward in my own directions. If you wrote this book, it would look a good bit different. If Neil Peart wrote it, it would look a lot different, I am sure. But in the most important sense the book is quite faithful to Rush's intent: Rush intends to provoke thought, not to spoon-feed their ideas to slavish fans who will not think for themselves.

Lyrics are only half the matter. Rush's music is just as evocative in its own way. It is really very remarkable music in fact, but I will not try to explain why. I am not a music critic in this sense. Another thing I am not is a biographer. I refer the reader interested in either the musicology or the biography of Rush to Bill Banasiewicz's fine book, *Visions: The Official Rush Biography* (Beekman Publications). There, the exemplary work of Geddy Lee and Alex Lifeson is paid due attention. Read it.

One last thing: my book contains not a single bit of backstage gossip. I really don't see the point of all that, and I can only speculate that so many Rock books are gossip books because there is nothing else to talk about. But with Rush there is much to talk about.

—Carol Selby Price

A RUSH CHRONOLOGY

1952 (Sept. 12) Neil Peart born at Hamilton, Ontario, Canada.

1953 (July 29) Gary Lee Weinrib (later Geddy Lee) born at Toronto, Ontario, Canada. (Aug. 27) Alex Zivojinovich (later Alex Lifeson) born at Surnie, British Columbia, Canada.

1969 John Rutsey (drums), Alex Lifeson (guitar), and Geddy Lee (bass, vocals) form Rush in Toronto, Canada.

1973 First album, *Rush*, appears on own label, Moon. Cleveland DJ Donna Halper tells Mercury Records, leading to contract.

1974 Reissue of *Rush* by Mercury. Rutsey leaves band, replaced by drummer-lyricist Neil Peart. First US tour.

1975 Second album, *Fly by Night* (March). Third album, *Caress of Steel* (November). Named Most Promising Group at Canadian Juno Awards.

1976 Fourth album, *2112* (May), featuring Hugh Syme on keyboard; fifth album, live performance, *All the World's a Stage* (November).

1977 First tour in Britain (June). Sixth album, *A Farewell to Kings* (October). Gold records awarded for *All the World's a Stage*, *2112*, and *A Farewell to Kings* (November).

1978 Best Group Award at Juno Awards (February). *Archives*, reissue of *Rush*, *Fly by Night*, and *Caress of Steel* (April). Seventh album, *Hemispheres* (December).

1979 Named "Official Ambassadors of Music" by Canadian Government; received Best Group Award at Juno Awards.

1980 Eighth album, *Permanent Waves* (February).

1981 Ninth album, *Moving Pictures* (March), featuring Hugh Syme on keyboards. *All the World's a Stage* earns platinum record. Tenth album, *Exit...Stage Left* (live performance, November).

1982 Geddy Lee joins Bob and Doug McKenzie on *Take Off* (March). Eleventh album, *Signals* (October), which goes platinum in November.

1984 Twelfth album, *Grace Under Pressure* (May), which goes platinum in June.

1985 Thirteenth album, *Power Windows*, featuring Andy Richard on keyboards (November).

1986 *Power Windows* goes platinum (January). Gold record for *Exit...Stage Left* (February).

1987 Fourteenth album, *Hold Your Fire*, with Aimee Mann adding vocals to "Time Stand Still" (November), which immediately receives gold record. Platinum record for *Exit...Stage Left* and *Permanent Waves* (November).

1989 Fifteenth album, *A Show of Hands* (live performance, January), which goes gold in March. *A Show of Hands* video goes platinum (June). Groups leaves Mercury for Atlantic with sixteenth album, *Presto* (December).

1990 Gold record for *Presto* (January). Mercury releases retrospective album, *Chronicles* (October).

1991 Seventeenth album, *Roll the Bones* (September), which goes gold in October. Golden Ticket Award at Madison Square Garden for selling more than 100,000 tickets there from 1981-1991.

1992 *Roll the Bones* named Best Hard Rock Album at Juno (April).

1993 Eighteenth album, *Counterparts*, with John Webster on keyboards (October). Gold records for *Caress of Steel* and *Counterparts*, platinum for *A Farewell to Kings*, *Fly by Night*, and *Hemispheres* (December).

1994 Peart releases *Burning for Buddy: A Tribute to the Music of Buddy Rich*; wins Buddy Rich Lifetime Achievement Award.

1996 Lifeson releases *Victor*. Nineteenth album, *Test for Echo*. *Working Man* album, a tribute to Rush, featuring their songs performed by other artists.

I.

FEAR

Rush fans scanning the lyrics printed on the jacket of *Moving Pictures* back in 1981 no doubt paused in puzzlement to notice that "Witch Hunt" was tagged "Part III of 'Fear.'" A quick memory bank check revealed no previous parts I and II of anything called "Fear," nor did a hasty thumbing through of album covers. But the next album, the next year, provided a clue: there was "Part II of 'Fear,'" namely "The Weapon" on the *Signals* album. And sure enough, *Grace Under Pressure* (1983) brought "The Enemy Within," "Part I of 'Fear.'" Let's take a closer look at the complete "Fear" trilogy, together with some related lyrics from other songs.

But first, why were the three released in reverse order? The answer is that Rush is trying to depict the phenomenon of fear in its origin and successive manifestations. The songs diagram fear in three concentric circles, so to speak. The outermost circle is the most apparent to outsiders, the one we would see first, yet it stems from whatever is inside. The three circles, the three songs, are like the wave pattern produced when you drop something into a pond: whatever created those outer-moving circles is at the center. To get to the root of fear, then, we must begin with its outward manifestation and work our way inward. That is why Part III appeared first. With each of the two albums thereafter we penetrate deeper into the jungle of fears, pressing on to the heart of darkness.

"Witch Hunt"

"Witch Hunt" opens with a scene that first reminds us of the typical mob scene in all those old monster films, the gathering of a posse of villagers hoisting aloft hoes, rakes, rifles, and torches, anything that lies ready at hand, to go and exterminate some insidious threat to the community. Is it the Frankenstein monster? No—or rather *yes!* Karloff's hulking harlequin was a symbol for anything that is frightening because of its *difference*. The persecuted giant stood for Jews, heretics, blacks, the retarded, freethinkers, martyrs, and pariahs of all ages and nations; even so, the vigilante mob in "Witch Hunt" could be any persecutors ready to persecute any victims. You can fill in the name of your favorite mob: the Neo-Nazis, the Ku Klux Klan, the Religious Rightists.

The song recounts a moonless night. These are vigilantes, no duly constituted authorities, so they must undertake their mission under cover of absolute darkness. They assemble atop a hill beyond the range of city lights, their torches the only illumination. They avoid the public square, because they shun the scrutiny of the law. This is not because they feel any shame or guilt for what they intend to do. Quite the contrary, in fact: they are perfectly still, untroubled by any pangs of regret or better judgment. At least in their own eyes it is the righteous who rise up. Why then act outside the law? All vigilante violence is moved by the belief that the official justice system is lax, inept, or corrupt. For whatever reason, the "proper authorities" cannot or will not do what needs to be done. The issues seem clearly drawn in the eyes of the lynch mob, and they mean to deal out stern justice. The police might differ, but the mob is calm in their right to do what they are about to do.

There are really three groups in view in "Witch Hunt." First, society at large, the "us" who are threatened by alien ways, the "us" who must be saved from ourselves. Society changes, as "Tom Sawyer" is well aware. He knows no particular change will be permanent, but that change itself is. Insofar as society is forward-looking it is open to change, new ideas, the participation of new groups in society. An open society is willing to listen, to learn, to assimilate, to change.

The second group is composed of the new social forces, the bringers of change, new immigrant groups (Japanese and Vietnamese in America, Pakistanis and Ugandans in England), new ideas (the Moonies, atheists, communists), new social styles (Rap, Reggae).

The third group is made up of the vigilantes. They see themselves as the conscience of the first group, and they seek to protect it from the corrupting inroads of the second group. It is the first group they seek to save, the second they intend to beat, burn, and kill. Like parents on the far side of the generation gap, the Witch Hunters are sure they know what's best for us, so they act on our behalf yet against our wishes.

Again, today's societies harbor many groups who seem to be competing for the role of the mob in this song. Notable examples from the recent past would include Germany's Nazis and America's Know-Nothing Party and KKK, both of which formed in the nineteenth century. The Klan is still around, and to their ranks we may add Great Britain's National Front. All these groups operated outside official power structures, with occasional attempts, sometimes successful, to seize the reins of power. All opposed the influx of immigrants (even if the immigrants, like Jews in Germany, had been there for centuries!), who usually had a different religion to boot.

To such organized racial and religious hate groups Rush's lyrics add book- and (we may suppose) record-burning mobs of today's fundamentalists (think of Khomeini's taking out a contract on *Satanic Verses* author Salman Rushdie), as well as those zealots who opposed "infidel" movies like *Monty Python's Life of Brian, Mohammad Messenger of God, Jesus of Nazareth, Hail Mary,* and *The Last Temptation of Christ.* What they really hate is *change.* In fact, anthropologists have a name for movements like these. They are called "revitalization movements." Khomeini's revolution in Iran was one such. The Moral Majority in America was another. They are confident their ways, the old, traditional ways, are best, and are eager to stop the hands of the clock, to prevent history from moving another step, to keep culture frozen.

From which of the three groups does the song proceed? It is not a protest from the persecuted, but rather from mainstream society which resents the efforts of those self-appointed to "save us from ourselves."

The narrative part of the song, the description of the assembling of the lynch mob, very adroitly uses the images of darkness and firelight to reveal how evil lies beneath the surface of pious intentions, obvious to everyone but the self-deceived mob itself. The darkness of the moonless night, in the eyes of the vigilantes, is a tactical shield making possible their righteous crusade, yet the rest of us see plainly that the mob gathers in darkness because they are creatures of darkness. "People loved darkness rather than light, because their deeds were evil" (John 3:19b). When the mob comes to arrest Jesus "with lanterns and torches and weapons" (John 18:3b), and to haul him off to a kangaroo court, what does he say to them, in a tone of cool irony? "Do you take me for a bandit, that you have come out with swords and clubs to arrest me? But this is your moment—the hour when darkness reigns" (Luke 22:52-53). How amazing that the Bible-pounding bigots of today cannot recognize themselves in this biblical scene! They *think* they do, but they are the mob, not Jesus.

The torches they will use to guide them in the night on their "holy" mission serve only to reveal their true, inner selves: the flickering firelight casts strange shadows over every face, making these hunters of a monster look like monsters themselves—which they are! The optical illusion of features "twisted and grotesque" reveals souls that are indeed "twisted and grotesque," as their actions are about to demonstrate, for how could the *righteous* beat, burn, and kill? The image of the mob's "burning eyes" calls up both a picture of eyes catching the firelight of the torches and a picture of wild eyes blazing with the inner magma of fanaticism, even madness, for they are madmen fed on fear and lies. Avenging angels in their own estimation, they are in reality a legion of demons, or of the demon-possessed.

15

The last three lines of the song name the demons possessing the mob. They are Ignorance, Prejudice, and Fear. The line between the vigilantes and the twisted spirits which move them is erased: the song began with a gathering, then marching mob; it closes with the unholy trinity of ignorance, prejudice, and fear walking hand in hand. These frightful specters walk with the mob; indeed, the mob incarnates them. These vigilantes *are* ignorance, prejudice, and fear stalking the land in human flesh.

Ignorance, prejudice, and fear support one another, depend upon each other. If one is ignorant of the strange-seeming ways of immigrants and infidels, what has one to rely on but inherited prejudices? Prejudices are "pre-judgments," the judgments we make on people or things before we know anything, really, about them. And it is a vicious circle, since your prejudices will make you reject, reinterpret, or explain away any contrary facts you encounter. And where does fear come in? Since the whole trilogy is named for it, Rush must view fear as the key ingredient. Fear of others, the primal emotion dating back to the early days of our evolution before laws or civilization existed to protect us from predators, leads us to embrace defensive prejudices. If your preconceptions about other races or religions make you steer clear of them, you will never get close enough to be either threatened or enriched by them. Fear constructs prejudices and forbids us to cast them aside.

Even so, many things would not seem fearsome if we were not ignorant about them, but fear keeps us far enough away that we never come to learn that our fears are unjustified. The mad mob in this song is afraid of strangeness, which it groundlessly fears to be "dangerous." Fear and fear-spawned lies feed their zealotry, egg them on to beat and burn and kill.

"The Weapon"

"The Weapon" is, quite simply, fear; fear is used to cow us, to subdue and to dominate us. How? We will see in a moment. By whom? In this second installment of "Fear" the kaleidoscope has been given a twist; the *dramatis personae* are not quite the same as in "Witch Hunt." Here the lunatic fringe of bigots and lynch mobs is no longer in view. Whereas "duly constituted" institutional authority was fairly benign in "Witch Hunt" (it wasn't the police, for example, who were doing the witch-hunting, but rather an outlaw mob), in "The Weapon" the establishment is viewed in a much more ominous light. Though it seems the establishment as a whole is accused here, Rush has chosen institutional religion as the instrument and perhaps as the figurehead for that establishment. Certainly the established Church has more than once felt entitled, moved by ignorance, prejudice, and fear, to beat, burn, and kill. Seven Crusades and the Inquisition of Medieval Europe give ample evidence of this. Yet, as we will see, it is not such overt oppression and persecution by religious authorities that the song warns of, but rather something much more insidious and dangerous.

The song begins with a nervous-sounding questioning of Franklin D. Roosevelt's dictum "We have nothing to fear, but fear itself." Is that so? Surely there are truly fearsome realities—possibilities for now, though realities sooner or later. Anyone's list would include pain, failure, fatal tragedy, the costly mistakes of others with roles of social responsibility, even romantic disappointments. Yes, these are fearsome things. But what stance, what attitude, to take in the meantime, until they strike us down? Shall we cower in fear and resignation? If we do surrender the fight before a single blow is struck, we are not even *waiting* for those terrors to do us in: we fall prey to their advancing shadows, even before they break the horizon. We yield in despair not to the fearsome realities but rather to phantom fears ("Free Will").

Or we might decide to venture out despite the lowering clouds of future death and disappointment, to gain as much ground as possible before we become another notch in the Reaper's scythe. We might exult, as does Jons the irreverent squire in Bergman's film *The Seventh Seal*, in the triumph of being alive even as the chill mist of death begins to gather. We might.

Or we might cop out and sell our souls to those who will trade empty promises of comfort for security and obedience. These are the religious authorities. They claim to protect us from the things we fear. Do we fear death? They will issue us a reserved ticket to Heaven. But the price is high: it is our freedom. We must do what the religious bigwigs command for fear of losing that ticket! There is Hell to pay if we stray from their kingdom's will. So it is an empty, fraudulent deliverance from fear that they promise. In fact, fear escalates. Fear of death becomes fear of an eternal Hell, and we come to fear our rescuers from fear more than anything else! What first seemed a smooth and comforting velvet glove is seen all too late to coat a brutal iron fist, and it is a thin coat at that. The shelter that seemed so secure, so welcome a haven against Shakespeare's "slings and arrows of outrageous fortune, the thousand natural shocks that flesh is heir to"—it turns out to be a shooting-gallery with you as the target. The cross atop the chapel of rest becomes the Sword of Damocles hanging tenuously above your head on a hair-thin cord. If we take refuge in religion, we are sheltered, all right, but under the gun.

The pious prayers we are taught become mantras to hypnotize us into a state of submissiveness. The conclusion of the Lord's Prayer, "Thy kingdom come, thy will be done...for thine is the kingdom, the power, and the glory, forever. Amen," becomes a hymn to the power of the rulers of the Church: merely a cynical glory game for the posturing princes and popes. "This train don't carry no sinners" to heaven, says the old spiritual, but you, poor mortal, are merely the baggage.

The paradox, the tragedy, is that, like the poor, abused sanitarium inmates in *One Flew Over the Cuckoo's Nest*, the inmates of the Church are free to leave any time they want to, and don't. Rush's picture of religion recalls Nietzsche's condemnation of Christianity as a "slave morality," the creed of the cringing cowardly herd, for whom "faith" can be defined as not wanting to know the truth, whose real fear is the fear of their own freedom, and whose greatest joy, masochistic though it be, is to "lay down the burden" of their *freedom* "down by the riverside." (Another Rush song, "Free Will," explicitly attacks this aspect of religion, astrology, and superstition.)

Walter Kaufmann makes the same point in his book *The Faith of a Heretic*:

> Those committed to an institution generally claim that all those who prefer fresh air and freedom lack the courage to commit themselves. In fact, the shoe is on the other foot. More often than not, commitment to an institution issues from a want of courage to stand alone. Typically, it is an excuse, a search for togetherness, for safety in numbers. Whether one joins the Communist party or the Catholic church, the Nazis or one of the Protestant denominations, the point may be, though it need not be, that one avoids the risk henceforth of sticking out one's neck, except in company.

Eric Hoffer's *The True Believer* explores this theme at length.

The Church and its leaders in "The Weapon" are just like the Grand Inquisitor in Dostoevsky's parable (in *The Brothers Karamazov*). In that story, Jesus appears on earth, among the peasants in Spain during the Inquisition. He is promptly locked up by the authorities of the Church! The chief heresy-hunter, or Grand Inquisitor, comes to interrogate Jesus. Why has Jesus made such a nuisance of himself, to come back like this and upset so many centuries of Church work? What mischief it had been for Jesus to come in the first place to challenge humanity to seek truth for themselves and not to be bamboozled by miracle-mongers, intimidated by powerful clergy! All he did was to frighten and upset the people, says the Inquisitor; people are like docile sheep. More than anything else they want a shepherd who will tell them precisely what to think, to do, to believe, one who will flatter and cajole, who will threaten Hell and promise Heaven. The Grand Inquisitor doesn't intend to let Jesus ruin things again! It's taken centuries to undo the damage he did the *first* time!

It is this Grand Inquisitorial Religion, this dispenser of what Marx called the opium of the people, that Rush condemns. But it is not sheer and simple victimization, and that is the crucial point. We have given the Church the very weapon it uses to enslave us! We told the Grand Inquisitor what we feared in life and after life, and he promised to protect us, but he will withdraw his protection and subject us to even more fearsome horrors if we dare to question him.

But the questioner, the doubter, the rebel against conventional religion, is championed in the third stanza. He scoffs at theological threats of judgment. Real life has shown that there are plenty of this-world horrors that make the mythical Hell of fire look like the fairy-tale it is. But what horrors could possibly be worse than Hell is supposed to be? The horror of a wasted life, a life crippled by fear, a life spent in cringing behind the walls of secure enslavement of the mind. Granted, death is fearsome (who after all, *isn't* at least a little bit afraid of dying?), but worse is life lived under the paralyzing but empty threats of the Grand Inquisitor.

What follows is a sample of the reasoning that alone can free us from the shackles of oppressive Religion. Rush poses questions intended to expose the absurdity of belief in an afterlife. Does the Church say your behavior in this life is worth eternal reward or punishment? How would a temporal, finite act have eternal, infinite consequences? A particular act, a crime or a sin, thus becomes mythically larger than life. Even love, which St. Paul says abides forever (I Corinthians 13:13), must be limited by time. So much for Heaven, and Hell seems no more likely. That is, how could it be justice to send even a murderer to suffer eternal torture in Hell? Wouldn't such a sentence be an even worse crime than he himself committed? That's making the killer worth more than his crime.

The Inquisitors of religion seem compassionate, but it's only skin-deep. Their pious prating about love lasts only as long as you're obeying them. Love and fear are opposites, and despite their scriptural sloganeering, the Grand Inquisitors really trade in fear. They live off the fears of their flock as a leech lives off blood.

Perhaps the greatest irony is that despite their cruel manipulation of others, the Inquisitors are just as much victims of fear as their victims! They are deceivers, true, but equally *self*-deceived. They do not know better. They believe their own lies about Heaven and Hell and hope most devoutly to negotiate the path between them. They themselves huddle behind the secure prison walls of ignorance. If the poor prisoners are there by choice, it is no less true that the wardens are just as much prisoners!

And there is one key to unlock this prison, one siege engine that can storm the walls: knowledge.

With "The Weapon," then, we are getting closer to the heart, we are penetrating to the core of fear. "Witch Hunt" ascribed the violence of bigots and the lunatic fringe to fear of the strange, fear of change. But "The Weapon" shows how the very security of that same mainstream society is a product of fear, too. It is not just the wild-eyed madmen whose fears push them to drastic action. Our safe position far from the fringe, in the midst of civilized, polite, secure society, is a cringing huddle of the fearful. Perhaps it is not change we fear—the strangeness in bookstores and theaters does not disturb us unduly—but it is fear of loss and failure that makes us retreat from adventure into safe and soul-killing convention. At least the madmen and vigilantes do not fear to act decisively. Aren't the rest of us, then, somehow worse? Even more pathetic? Where is the real enemy? Who is it? The fanatics might limit our freedom; they pose some threat. The establishment limits our freedom, but it is we who have given them permission to do it! So who is really to blame? Now we are ready to go right to the heart of the matter.

"The Enemy Within"

"The Enemy Within" is Part I of the Fear Trilogy in that it lays bare where the fear begins. It is part one because it is the beginning of the fear process which eventuates in slavery to institutions (and to destructive fanaticism when familiar institutions seem threatened). Part three of Fear depicted three groups in society: the lunatic fringe, the social mainstream, and the persecuted pariahs. In part two, the lunatics dropped out of view as we saw that mainstream society with its institutions is equally a refuge of fear, only less overtly dangerous. The persecuted dropped out at this stage, too, since the focus shifted to the oppression of individuals by the institutions to whom they yield control. In this jail who is the jailor? It is we ourselves. That is the point of this "first" part of "Fear."

Patrick McGoohan portrayed precisely the same view of things in the finale of his television series, *The Prisoner*. Through the previous sixteen episodes, the Prisoner fought to preserve his individual integrity in an insulated, isolated society called The Village, where every effort was made to win his conformity, his collaboration. The show was a great parable of individualism. In the last episode, "Fall Out," he is finally declared the winner: the System itself recognizes him to have beaten the System, whereupon he is offered the position of the new Number One, mastermind of The Village.

He is undecided, but goes to meet the incumbent Number One, a mysterious figure unseen and unknown throughout the whole series. Number One is a masked figure. The Prisoner rips away the mask—and sees his own face! We ourselves create our prison, are our jailors, demand our own conformity! Because the real enemy is the enemy within: our own fears.

The focus has narrowed in "The Enemy Within": there is only the individual. There at first seem to be external foes or dangers, but there are none. The things that seem to crawl in the darkness are really but ghosts draped in shrouds spun by our fear-fevered imaginations. The fearful imagination spins its webs of dread and crawls like spiders across your skin.

The second stanza depicts a person aroused in the "fight or flight" response to perceived danger. Blood pounds in the temple pulses! Adrenalin pours into the bloodstream! Muscles tense up! Gooseflesh! Nape hairs prickle! You are ready to square off with the enemy! But where is the intruder? He is within. "We have met the enemy, and he is us," Pogo said.

Skip to stanza five for more of the same: your tongue has the acrid taste of fear that horror novelists are always talking about, while you try to maintain a front of steely-eyed ferocity as if to make some attacker think twice. But the only attacker is your own fear, the very fright that makes you assume such a defensive posture.

The lesson Rush would teach here is a difficult one to swallow. If there are no external enemies, one might think that by process of elimination we would have to face the fact—the enemy is within. But no, if there are no enemies out there, we will begin to create them. The previous stanza shows paranoia in action. A stranger arouses your suspicions when he shows you a dangerous grin, but this stranger's grinning face is only a mirror reflecting back to you your own suspicions of danger.

If we must finally face up to the fact that FDR was right after all, that "The only thing we have to fear is fear itself," whence that fear? What are we afraid of? There is something frightening, something intimidating about the promise of adventure, about implausible dreams. It is not the prospect of the adventure itself that we find so daunting, as Bilbo Baggins did in Tolkien's *The Hobbit*, as if we feared sacrifices or dangers that following a dream might entail. No, it is rather the possibility of *failure*.

At all costs we want to hold on to some vestige of self-esteem. We think we might possess the potential for great things, great adventures—else why would the dream of them tempt us? But what if the concrete *attempt* proves we are wrong, shows that after all we lack what it requires? That we cannot abide. So, we tell ourselves, it is better to rest content with daydreams which at least allow the pleasant belief that we *might* have in us what it takes, much better than to risk all on the venture that will prove us, try us, tell us what we are made of. So we hang back.

So we seek security under pressure, respite from the pressure, where we can be "safe" and dry and listen to the pounding rain on the roof. The pounding is the pressure of possibility, the insistent reminder of conscience telling us we are faking it. Martin Heidegger said that we flee the terrible risk of personal "authenticity" and take refuge in a kind of "lowest common denominator" existence. We lose all sensation by lowering ourselves into the tepid tank of body-temperature water, conformity, security, soullessness, copping out. But if we stay there in the shed of "security" long enough, we will grow accustomed to the pounding of possibility, the pressure of nagging conscience telling us we are not venturing to fulfill what we could be. Like the familiar ticking of the clock on the mantel, soon we will not even notice it any longer.

Precisely where are you taking this refuge? Not in the Church of the Grand Inquisitor, as in "The Weapon." No, "The Enemy Within" describes a prior and more fundamental capitulation without which the subsequent surrender to socio-religious conformity would not be possible.

You, out of the fear within you, the fear of discovering you do not measure up to your own dreams, are surrendering to an inner jailor, an inner Grand Inquisitor, a sane and calm and mundane you who would never think of challenging life, challenging the norm. It is the "grownup" self to which the fresh childlike self one day surrenders. And when we do, the world grows comfortable, but its colors dim, its sights and sounds blur, its flavors dull, and we hibernate.

Colin Wilson puts it well when he says that each person has within himself a "robot," a subconscious behavior pattern according to which experiences become second nature, and we do things without thinking or feeling, on automatic pilot. Of course, having this "automatic pilot" capability is an indispensable convenience. Would you really want the task of tying your shoes to absorb all your attention every time you do it? Isn't it much handier to be able to let your robot self do it while your mind is creatively engaged elsewhere? Of course, but we are in danger of letting the robot take over *all* our living. Soon we find it is much easier to have conversations with our friends or our spouse while on automatic pilot. When we engage in the rituals of small talk and polite chitchat, isn't this precisely what we are doing? "Oh, robot, here comes that bore Jones. Entertain him, will you?, while I think about what I'm to do tomorrow." But if the robot takes over all of waking life, the soul sinks into a lazy snooze. Life becomes stale and dull, and we become used to the torpor.

Wilson charges that most people in society have surrendered once and for all to their robot selves. About five percent seem to recognize what is happening and seek to shock themselves out of the state Pink Floyd calls being "comfortably numb." These are the artistic creators, the leaders, the saints and mystics—even the murderers and serial killers, for some shake themselves awake too violently. All these Wilson calls "Outsiders," because their escape from robotic existence distances them from the common run of humanity.

Plato's Allegory of the Cave made this clear. He told of an imaginary cave society where all was dim and people saw only shadows, until one day one man escapes and finds his way up to the surface. There he sees sunlight for the first time and beholds all things in their true and vivid colors. He goes back down to invite his fellow cave-dwellers to join him on the surface, but he meets only skepticism and derision. So accustomed are they to the shadows that they cannot believe, do not really want to believe, that greater light exists. But having been enlightened, the man can never go back. He knows too much. As in Kansas's song "Carry On Wayward Son," he has gone beyond this illusion. He is an Outsider.

Wilson, a self-professed Outsider himself, knows it is no easy task to remain free of robotism. What is the secret? "The Outsider's salvation lies in extremes." That is, in daring living. Not recklessness, not foolish, self-destructive behavior, but rather living at the extreme of *effort*, doing nothing half-heartedly, weak-willedly. Living at the extreme of personal honesty in dealings with others, being open to the extremes of pleasure or pain that life brings you when you live it to the full, shirking no opportunity for self-growth and self-testing.

Isn't it apparent that Rush is calling listeners of "The Enemy Within" to shut the robot off, to abandon their sleepy security, to become Outsiders? What is "Tom Sawyer," after all, but an archetypal Wilsonian Outsider? He has resolved not to prostitute his convictions, not to rent out his allegiance to any religious or political idol. Why? Because he has already conquered "The Enemy Within," namely *fear*. He has won this victory by resolving to take experience to extremes, the same formula Wilson prescribes: "The Outsider's salvation lies in extremes."

Why is it such a fight? Because of what we have concealed under "Lock and Key," all sorts of volatile cargo below the water line, like carrying nitroglycerin on a bumpy ride, as in the movie *Wages of Fear*. It is the brash, fresh instinctive part of you that yearns, that aches to experience in full flood tide. "Lock and Key" focuses on "the killer instinct" and our fear that, along with our other animal urges, it will get out of hand, so for the sake of security we suppress and repress the living, vibrant, animal courage, and substitute the tepid, torpid, vapid, but secure robotic, mechanistic, automatic-pilot self. Risk is the price of being free, and we'd rather not pay it. After all, even Wilson admits some Outsiders don't know how to handle the explosion of freedom and become psychopaths.

Of course, Rush is not advocating this kind of experience taken to extremes. Their point is simply that for fear of the explosive, volatile nature of the real self, one leaves it buried. Their point is to get you, the listener, to wake up, turn off the robot.

Have you done so? You think you have; after all, aren't you an aficionado of this band whose lyrics are about ideas, not about drugs and hormones? But Rush presses the question: what do you do in a day—is it mere movement, something done on automatic pilot? Or is it action, what Sartre would call an "authenticating act," a deed that "authenticates your existence" because it is the free and chosen act of an individual taking a stand?

How about your daily encounters with other people? Are you making genuine contact? A meeting of minds, an "I-Thou encounter" (Martin Buber)? Or are you just reacting like the stimulus-response mechanism that behaviorist psychologist B. F. Skinner said you are? Are you just *existing*, like a machine does? Or really *living*, like a human self? Your options are revolution or mere resistance—will you make the decisive break with the robot? The robot is the enemy within, and fear is the electricity that makes him run.

Fear of the new and the strange, fear of an imaginary Hell, finally, fear of one's own potential greatness, lest it turn out not to be great enough. These are the concentric circles of fear. To understand them we must move from the periphery to the center. If we remain in circle one and self-righteously put the blame on the lynch mob of witch-hunters, if we linger in circle two and make the Grand Inquisitor the villain, we will never defeat the real fear-monger, the enemy within. Once that Goliath lies headless in the dust, the Inquisitors and the witch-hunters can neither claim our allegiance nor scare us with their threats.

II.

THE MASS PRODUCTION ZONE

Rush's antidote for fear is hope and dreams; Neil Peart's prescription for conformity is courage. The assumption is that there are no natural herd members, that every individual can and should embrace the glory, the destiny, the risk of individuality. It takes courage to be what you really are: an individual with a destiny revealed to you by your own dreams. These themes so thoroughly pervade Rush's music that it is almost an arbitrary choice as to which particular songs we will discuss to illustrate them. A good place to start is with "Grand Designs" (*Power Windows*, 1985) and "The Body Electric" (*Grace Under Pressure*, 1984). We will consider the two songs in logical, not chronological, sequence. This way we can see first the challenge of breaking with society's mass production scheme in broad outline, and then we will be in a position to see more clearly the real root of that oppressive system and just how great are the odds the would-be individual truly faces. We will consider several other songs along the way.

"Grand Designs"

"Grand Designs?" Whose, pray tell? This song implies that you are a work in progress, being shaped and formed in accordance with *some* norms—but whose? The issue here is *social conforming*, and not in the trivial sense of clothing or hair styles (indeed the social flap in the Sixties over these externals served merely to distract attention from the *real* issues of conformity, those of the unspoken values and assumptions tacitly shared by hippies and hardhats alike). No, this song, these words, are all about what Heidegger called "inauthentic existence." The song, whether Peart was consciously thinking of him or not, fairly screams "Heidegger" to the reader in the know.

Amid the prevailing climate of style with no substance (there are those clothing and hair "issues" again), in the midst of a flood of unrefined stuff with no style, where is authenticity? As we hear in "Vital Signs," everybody's got mixed feelings about the function and the form. That is, in our crazy North Atlantic society, all is either an exercise in vacuous style with nothing behind it (the great fixation of the Eighties, from the Reagan presidency to flashy *Miami Vice*) or

25

hideously ugly functionalism, like the identical, monotonous housing complexes of Rush's *Subdivisions* video. An authentic product would perfectly wed function and form, use and beauty. They had an eye for such things in the Victorian period. But in our time, it's hard to recognize the real thing, *not* because it looks so much like the unreal thing, the fake, but rather because one so seldom sees it (it comes along *only* every once in a while), and finally one comes to stop looking out for it. After a while one begins to doubt that anything better, anything good, ever existed. One fatally lowers one's horizons, limits one's perspective.

But more than aesthetics is going on here, much more. Because *you* are the product on the designing board! Society's commercial and political engineers are sketching you out according to their own blueprint. And if they have their way, you will be simply one more piece of fluff or of useful junk—in any case serving their interests and easily disposable. If against all odds, you are to emerge from the designing table and the assembly line as "the real thing," it will be because you somehow managed to grab the pencil, the compass, and the T-square, and to design yourself according to grander norms.

Heidegger in *Being and Time* wrote of the state of "inauthentic existence" in which each of us finds himself or herself. It is a stage of "fallenness." Deep down we know we are capable of better. And precisely what is *wrong*? What have we fallen into? *Conformity*. And the evil of conforming is *abdication*. We are happy to be absolved of the duty to forge our own values, to make our own decisions, to bear the responsibility for their consequences. Who will blame us, who will trouble us, if we take refuge in the mass-existence of the herd, speaking, buying, voting, and believing in accordance with the herd? Public opinion, inherited values, political slogans, and religious dogmas substitute for our own critical thinking. And we, lazy slugs, are only too happy to surrender. We loyally march in lock-step conformity with the mass, the collectivity, what Heidegger calls *das Mann*, more or less the idea of the faceless "John Q. Public." Such existence is inauthentic, it is copping out; we were intended for better things.

Rush says the real thing is buried, like gold ore or a diamond beneath a ton of rock. That means two things: first, it's worth finding; second, it's not going to be easy. Start digging. In practical terms, this means a lot of listening to a lot of useless talk. Of course, the point is not that if you listen to a sufficient amount of useless talk the sheer volume will somehow do the trick. No, you have to hear enough of it to realize, finally, why it is so useless. And that is because you are listening to *others*—other sold-out conformists, other cookie-cutter compromisers, other happy herd-members. The talk that will be useful, useful for liberation, is the talk you can hear, if you listen hard enough, *from within*.

Socrates learned this lesson, just as Peart says, by listening to a lot of windy talk. You see, a friend of his had asked the Oracle of Delphi who was the wisest man in all Athens. The prophetess replied, "Socrates." Socrates simply could not believe his ears! Why, he must rank well behind dozens of Athenian businessmen and politicians, to say nothing of priests and philosophers! So he set out to prove the Delphic Oracle wrong. He decided to interview some of Athens's leading citizens. It shouldn't take but a few minutes to refute the Oracle, he reasoned. All he need do was to ask a few questions about virtue, truth, and the good life. The answers he would get should more than prove that Athens was filled with men wiser than he. Poor Socrates was in for a shock! He found them all, without exception, to be the worst kind of pompous windbags, "full of sound and fury, signifying nothing" (as Shakespeare put it). The realization gradually forced itself upon Socrates that he was after all the wisest man in Athens because he alone realized he was not *wise*. The others *thought* they *were* when they *weren't! He* wasn't, but he *knew* it, and *that* put him well ahead of *them!*

In his long career as the pest and troublemaker of Athens, Socrates learned to listen to his inner *daimon*, or genius. His whole teaching method, the "midwife" method, was designed to draw forth the truth from where it already *is—within* each person. But the process of excavating this inner truth is no easy one, as Plato's records of Socrates's many dialogues show clearly. A series of probing questions gradually unlock, disclose, uncover the truth within.

And now this song returns to Heidegger. He said the only way to come to your senses, to snap out of the pleasant but deadening torpor of fake existence is to listen to that faint voice of conscience, the lingering memory of what you really are. Heidegger called it "the call."

Why is it so faint? Because we can barely hear its call above the programmed slogans and dogmas and maxims and catechisms reverberating through our skulls. The loudspeakers of society and its masters are as ever-present, ever-vigilant as Big Brother in George Orwell's *Nineteen Eighty-Four*. But it is in our power to click off the volume, if we have the courage, and to listen to the still, small voice of our own identity.

What will happen if we do? If we make the conversion over to *authentic* existence? If we design *ourselves?* It will be a revelation, like the religious revelations of old, and that revelation is a revealing *of* oneself, *from* oneself, *to* oneself!

We hear next of shapes and forms that are somehow construed as being against the norm. Let's compare these evocative lines with a matching sentiment from "Vital Signs," where we hear that everybody must elevate themselves above the norm. Here we can see an implicit reference to Buddhism, or a spontaneous parallel to it. The Buddhist yoga of the Eightfold Path maps out a method of focusing consciousness so as to escape this dreary, frustrating system called *Samsara,* an endless treadmill on which our very thirst for inherently unsatisfying mirages makes us gluttons for punishment. As long as we persist in the delusion that this illusory system of worldly existence holds promise for us, we will keep getting reborn into it. What we need to do, as in Kansas's song "Carry On Wayward Son," is to get beyond this illusion. And as one is going ever higher, the Buddhists say, one's consciousness rises beyond *namarupa,* the level on which one perceives "name and form," worldly categories (Rush's shapes and forms). One sees them as the phantoms they are, and one ceases to desire them. One desires only liberation. And such an awakening is to transcend, ascend above the norm.

Now it may not be a quest for mystical absorption (though, then again, as in "Tai Shan," it may be), but to live authentically one must swim against the current, go against the run of the mill, *i.e.,* beyond the standard product stamped out on the assembly line, beyond the parameters of society's mass-production scheme. You see, true, authentic human beings *cannot be mass-produced!* What *can* be? If not humans, then *humanoids,* but we are getting ahead of ourselves and into the next song!

How has life become a mass-production scheme? The lyrics of "Grand Designs" speak of principles being left out of the formula, the exclusion of the spirit because of the preponderance of the mind: ironically, we can put so much mind on the matter that the spirit is simply forgotten. This theme will concern us again in Chapter VII, "Machine and Man," but here let's pause to note that Heidegger would say "Amen!" He drew precisely the same distinction in his small book, *On What Is Called Thinking.* He says our industrial-scientific society is well trained in "calculative thinking," but out of practice when it comes to "meditative thinking." We live too much in the left brain, not enough in the right brain. We tackle technical problems, but remain oblivious to the great mysteries of existence which can be discerned only with the spirit, with intuition.

Efficiency is the great goal of a calculative, machine-like society which creates the depersonalizing evils of both Capitalist and Communist systems: people are no longer souls, ends in themselves, but mere things, quanta, commodities, and consumers, thus expendable. The lack of spirit in social-economic planners, the omission of that righteous inspiration which was overlooked in haste, is the insidious poison in power. Both of the philosophies, Marxism and Capitalism, are certainly among those worldviews that are not *spacious, i.e.,* full of room to recognize the various aspects of human life, but rather merely *spaced*—delusional.

It is in the interest of a society that worships Efficiency to preserve the status quo, to avoid rocking the boat, to keep things as they are. And to ensure that result, you and I *must be inauthentic:* we must not listen to "the call" of our buried identity, but rather must want and buy what Big Brother tells us to want and buy. And why not? It's all so much easier that way! How placid, how calm and unruffled is the glasslike surface of the lake—*if we don't make waves*. But make waves we must if we are to live authentically, if we are to dive deep to find the lost treasure, the real thing. The surface tension of the pond seems to hold placidly until we shatter the glassy-smooth surface with the eruption of our wild, thrashing dreams. These are the dreams of the living, moving, wild, and rejoicing beings we really are if we have the courage to be.

"The Body Electric"

"The Body Electric" implies all that we have seen in "Grand Designs," only here things have gone farther. The human addressed in "Grand Designs" is pictured here. "Grand Designs" told the listener one must get off Society's designing table before he can be successfully transformed into an obedient social robot. "The Body Electric" observes one such robot, a compliant consumer and conformer who amazingly *still manages* to hear the call of his buried identity, still almost manages to remember who he was, and struggles to become authentically human.

The title, "The Body Electric," comes from Walt Whitman's poem, "I Sing the Body Electric." This long lyric is a hymn to the beauty and glory of every human body. Why "electric?" Because, Whitman says, all bodies are "charge[d]—full with a charge of the soul." Whitman meant to reject the classical division between body and soul. For a long time many religious and philosophical thinkers saw the body as no more than a vehicle, a beast of burden carrying around its master, the mind or soul. Against this Whitman championed the body. "And if the body were not the soul, what is the soul?" That is, the soul is not some ghost imprisoned in the inert heap of the body; it is the animating force that makes the body alive and beautiful. The soul, or *anima* (in Latin), is the animation *of the body*. Whitman went on to celebrate the lines and shapes of the body, all that it is and does. Humble humanity is godlike, and not at all to be despised.

Neil Peart has taken the same phrase, the same image, to describe the total ruination of humanity, its corruption and degradation via the mass-production scheme. People are mere fodder for the commercialistic machine that will grind them up and make them into submissive units of society, subservient to its purposes. Here, "the body electric" denotes that the godlike temple of flesh celebrated by Whitman has become a *machine*, a mechanical man, a humanoid, or android. The prefix "andro" simply means "man" in Greek, and the suffix "-oid" just means "-like," so "humanoid" and "android" both mean a machine that is remarkably like a human being, yet not *quite* human. What's the difference? The android is as close to human as suits its master's desires. It performs those, and only those, human tasks that are useful for the intelligence that controls it. What's missing is *initiative, free will*, spirit. As we heard in "Grand Designs," the spirit gets lost in the mass-production scheme, as the humanoid robots roll off the assembly line.

As "The Body Electric" begins we seem to be viewing, as from far above, perhaps from a helicopter or a surveillance satellite, the spectacle of a lone figure running in no particular direction across a desert waste. He is not making for any place in particular; he just wants to leave his point of origin far behind. Where is this figure, who perhaps now and again stumbles and falls? And where is it running from? It is a futuristic, science fiction scenario. We are to imagine a world scorched and parched, able to support life only in underground or domed shelters. Perhaps we find ourselves in the aftermath of a nuclear war which rendered the surface of the earth largely uninhabitable. Since resources are few, population must be strictly controlled, and that in two ways. First, numbers must be kept down to a manageable size. Second, *behavior*, even *thoughts*, must be controlled and thus rendered manageable. Rebellion is a luxury unaffordable in such a world, where all efforts are aimed at stemming the tide of chaos, keeping a livable order. If rebellion is a luxury, freedom is a risk, because it might lead to rebellion. Hence human life has been radically reduced in quality as well as quantity. All survivors are reduced to manageable zombies for the sake of the common good.

All this is implied, effectively painted with minimal strokes in the first four lines: a single humanoid makes a headlong dash for freedom across a blackened desert expanse. But why is he fleeing the humanoid hive? Why take his chances in the wilderness beyond the plexiglass dome, where security was his? Because somehow he has come to realize that the environment within the dome is as much a desert as that outside it. The lack of freedom, of spirit, is just as deadly as the lack of water, perhaps more so, more to be feared. The waterless desert outside abounds in freedom and so, from within the dome, the desert comes to seem like the Oasis of Eden. He makes his break.

But again we have to ask, how could such an insight occur to this "humanoid," this "android," in the first place? The theme of the artificial intelligence of a robot blossoming into a true human soul is a familiar theme in the pages of science fiction, at least from the Tin Woodman in L. Frank Baum's *The Wizard of Oz*, through the Robotrix of Fritz Lang's *Metropolis* and Otto Binder's *Adam Link, Robot*, to Lieutenant Commander Data of *Star Trek: The Next Generation*. But Rush is using the theme as an allegory, along the lines of "Grand Designs." Society has made us into obedient robots by programming us to buy and vote like good little automatons.

Do you think this is paranoid? Think of advertising, and how Madison Avenue cynically exploits the desperate need of adolescents for peer approval. The admen know that it means big money if they can get everyone to follow a fashion or a fad. Remember the designer jeans craze in the late Seventies? You were a leper and a pariah if your rear was not laminated in the latest brand of circulation-choking denims. So everybody raced to be first in line to wear the "in" designer label on their buttocks. Like the damned in the Book of Revelation lining up to get branded on the butt with the Mark of the Beast, kids would sell their souls for a pair of Jordache jeans. And then, lo and behold, one day advertisers blew the whistle and unveiled a commercial where somebody sings "Love my *baggy* jeans!" Into the mothballs with the skin-tight zip suits, into the stores, wallets emptying to buy a few expensive pairs of baggies! Who should we consider the founder of modern advertising, do you suppose? Pavlov, with his dogs conditioned to salivate on cue? Or Hitler's propaganda minister, Josef Goebbels? A toss-up.

Is politics any better? Elections are won by sound-bites and slogans and TV commercials that avoid issues like one would avoid the Black Death, focusing on "feel-good" moods and tones instead (so much style without substance). And the mass media do your thinking for you. Do you realize that in every American presidential election there are actually dozens of parties and candidates? Yet you will only hear the names of two or at most three candidates, because TV has decided that you needn't take the Socialist, the Libertarian, the Communist, and other candidates seriously. If this isn't programming, what word would you use for it? If you never think to question any of this, what word besides "robot" would you consider appropriate?

To a great degree, all political philosophy is a debate over just who should program the rest of us, who gets to play Big Brother. In America it's Big Business. In China it's the Party. In Iran it's the clerics. B. F. Skinner, in his frightening books *Beyond Freedom and Dignity* (the title says it all!) and *Walden Two*, proposed that society be controlled by psychological specialists who would run the world like one big "Skinner box." Since, Skinner reasoned, all of us are just more complicated pigeons and lab-rats, and our behavior the predictable sum of stimulus-plus-response, then the solution to society's ills is to let behaviorist bigwigs manipulate the rest of us. Can Huxley's *Brave New World* be far behind? Just machines to make big decisions, Donald Fagen's satirical prophecy tells us, machines programmed by fellas with compassion and vision.

Rush's humanoid escapee has somehow managed to penetrate the programming. It knows that the chains that bind it to a robotic existence are those inside: the careful programming it long ago received from its masters. Now it strives to reprogram itself, to dredge up a long-submerged program called "free will." At first only chaotic, conflicting images, fragments from that earlier programming appear, and they clash with the control-commands of his masters. Propelled like a flung rag-doll by the interior explosion, the android struggles to gain control, clenching his plastic humanoid fist in a last gesture of defiance. Even if he must self-destruct, he will deprive the masters of the mass-production zone of their drone.

The humanoid struggles to become human, to shake loose from the programming, to stop listening, stop paying attention to the images he's been fed for years. The resulting static is a kind of cross-circuited schizophrenia. Whose voice to obey? Can he even hear the call of his humanness over the propaganda loop of his masters?

But it's beginning to work! The memory banks unload, dumping the years of directives. The computer-brain's memory-bytes break into bits, clearing the program. But can the humanoid, now the human, reprogram himself? Freedom is scary; our newly reborn human is scared out of his wits as he teeters on the brink of the yawning chasm of freedom (see the discussion of the "Fear Trilogy" in the previous chapter).

To *exist* as an autonomous being is to *resist* the guidance systems imposed upon the self from outside. It is to clench one's plastic fist in rebellion, for only so will it turn slowly back into flesh. The humanoid escapee begins to exist, to experience authentic existence, in the moment he begins to resist.

If political philosophy is the debate over who will control us, Plato had one of the most striking suggestions. In *The Republic*, Plato spun out an elaborate parable, The Allegory of the Cave, which we invoked briefly in the previous chapter. Let's return to it now in a bit more detail. Imagine a bizarre underground chamber, almost a kind of torture chamber really. In it live captives, born and bred there, who know of no better form of existence. As if their imprisonment were not enough, each cave-dweller is chained to the spot in such a way that he or she can only face forward. Straight ahead each sees an elaborate shadow play. Behind the row of immobile viewers is a tier across which the captors carry two-dimensional cutouts in the shapes of common objects (horses, trees, people), and the shadows of these objects are projected by a huge fire onto the walls in front of the prisoners. This is all they have seen all their lives! They do not so much as suspect the existence of a third dimension! They have never dreamt of sunlight—or of freedom.

One day, Plato bids us imagine, a prisoner escapes and gains the upper world. He is bewildered, even terrified by what he sees there! Lights! Color! Depth! The true realities of which he had before seen only the vague shadows! At first the strong sunlight blinds his dark-accustomed eyes. But when he grows used to it he comes to rejoice in the higher level of reality he has attained to. At length he remembers his fellow hostages back in the cave and determines to lead them to freedom. Making his way back down the shaft to the cave he pleads with his companions to come back with him, but his words fall on deaf ears! They can only laugh in disbelieving scorn at the silly notions of three-dimensional, multicolored reality! He must return alone. What was Plato getting at? We are the prisoners in the cave. Our beliefs and opinions are merely distorted shadows of the truth. Can it be otherwise when supermarket tabloids like *The National Enquirer* are the largest selling periodicals? Surely people are floating in a sea of delusion! The philosopher, the enlightened person, alone sees the shining realm of Truth above this shadow world, and he or she must try to lead the masses to the same enlightenment. Or if this proves impossible, the philosopher would certainly be in a better position than anyone else to know how to govern the cave-prisoners, the ignorance-prisoners. Thus Plato proposed that philosopher-kings control society, not capitalist bosses, not party hacks, not religious mullahs, not behaviorist psychologists.

Where does this fit into "The Body Electric"? It is not difficult to see the humanoid escapee—bewildered and disoriented beneath the bright sun, yet exulting in the freedom it brings—as Plato's escapee from the controlled environment of the cave. In both cases, the sunlight symbolizes sudden enlightenment and the initial pain it brings as one struggles to free oneself from the programmed illusions of the past. Rush's songs, this one included, are attempts to persuade cave-prisoners to come out and risk exposure to the sunlight of knowing for yourself and deciding for yourself. Rush wants to see every person be his own philosopher-king, her own philosopher-queen. Why not? It's frightening, but maturity is always frightening. Emerge from the cave, emerge from the herd, break with the pack!

By the end of the song we see our escapee finally having tapped into the new source of guidance he will need if he is to live henceforth as a human. He prays to the mother of all machines—*the human mind, reason*! The song thus ends on a note of irony as well as hope. Human intelligence created the machines and the machine-like society which eventually succeeded in reducing humans themselves to mere *components*, mere cogs. To escape this self-created trap, one must skip the machines and the systems, and instead go right back to the source: reason and understanding. Forget what the artificial intelligence of the much-vaunted computer tells you to do! You once told *it* what to do, and you can tell it again!

But this song is not just about technology, any more than it is really about robots. Rather, the dome-city in the desert, a computer-controlled "brave new world," is an allegory like Plato's cave. It stands for society, just as "the mill," the assembly line, did in "Grand Designs." In itself, society is a vast machine that was created to serve us, but which we now serve. Sociologists call this process "reification." As Thomas Luckmann and Peter Berger tell it in their fascinating book, *The Social Construction of Reality*, the process works like this:

Human beings are unlike lower animals whose instincts automatically adjust them to their environment. We have intelligence instead of instinct. Our remote ancestors *chose* how best to adjust to their environment, how to meet its challenges. They created language, society, institutions for child-rearing, justice-administration, etc. They created these things to serve them, to make life easier. But they soon discovered that, like farm animals, institutions need to be fed, to be served. They tend to become greater than the human individuals for whose sake they were created, and, several generations down the line, we wind up serving, sacrificing, compromising, selling out for the sake of the system—which we ourselves did *not* create but only inherited! To rectify the injustice implied in this situation, Thomas Jefferson said every generation ought to stage its own revolution, recreate its own institutions that will be more appropriate to the new world each generation lives in.

Yet the cycle will continue. Reason, the mother of all machines, will continue to give birth, and one day another humanoid will have to make a break for it from another dome. This, again, was the stinging irony in the last episode ("Fall Out") of the TV series, *The Prisoner*. When his captors offer the Prisoner the rule of the Village, the viewer thinks: "Here is his chance! Here is his opportunity to reshape the Village into a free society!" But when he was finally escorted to meet the *old* ruler he found himself staring into his *own face!* It is an endless cycle! No doubt the previous Number One came into office with "grand designs" of humanizing the Village, but the constraints of power quenched those hopes (again, the poison in power chokes out the spirit). Only as the struggling *individual* can the humanoid become human. There is no authentic existence in the herd. You cannot exist without resisting. The minute you "go with the flow," you effectively cease to exist.

Yet we must have societies. Even if we are foredoomed to some measure of failure, we can strive to improve on what we inherited. And Rush calls on its listeners to get ready for their turn at bat, their generation's revolution, as Jefferson would say. Soon we will consider the dossier, the résumé, the portrait of the freed humanoid who will try to remake his world, today's Tom Sawyer. But first, let's take a look at an interconnected series of songs that sketch our dilemma from something of a different angle.

"Subdivisions"

"Subdivisions" (*Signals*, 1982) brings home to many young Rush listeners that face of conformity that they most often see: the anonymity of the suburbs. Here the forces toward conformity are two.

First is the very structure of suburban life, with its limiting, stifling options. Second is the gravity of peer-pressure that is so hard to defy.

Suburbia sprawls on the fringes of the city, laid out tidily in geometric order. It forms an insulated border between the city's bright lights and that which is far away, unlit and unknown. At first glance there seems to be a contradiction between the description of suburbia in the first line and that in the second. "Sprawling" implies a random, rank growth; it leaves us with the image of an unregulated weed patch at the edge of a garden. Yet immediately this description is qualified; with geometric order, the suburbs are rigidly and systematically planned out. Which is it? Or can it be both? Actually the suburbs *are* both, and it is nothing new to recognize it. Since the 1950s sociologists have spoken of "suburban sprawl" and no less of the carefully "manicured lawns" of suburbia. The seeming contradiction is resolved once one grasps the logic of the suburbs. They are a safety net against the dangers of the city's bright lights. People have had enough of the fast pace of city life, the actual physical dangers there, the multi-ethnic kaleidoscope of customs and morals, the watermain breaks, the riots, the boom-box radios blaring Rap music. The suburbs sprawl because they are a buffer, an insulated border. People have poured out of the cities with all the speed they could muster, and more do it all the time, so the borders of the suburbs sprawl. Their shape is uncertain and ever-shifting because they bounce with the impact of hurtling commuters, they expand with new residents, pushing further into the countryside, or into what used to be small towns.

But once urban refugees settle in, they create a world as full of order, regularity, and humdrum security as the city was empty of these things. One extreme begets its opposite. If the city was chaotic, it was at least a creative chaos from whose seething primal stew anything might emerge. The suburbs are geometrically ordered so as to eliminate the last shadow of chaos—but nothing can grow in their sterility. If the city was bewildering in its diversity, at least it presented a range of options. The suburbs are block-on-block, town-on-town the same. With numbing monotony, each suburb looks the same, and only "Welcome to Levittown" signs tell you when you've passed from one into another.

It's like the repeating landscape in the background animation of a cartoon. Ever notice how when Popeye or Bugs Bunny is riding a train at high speed you start to see the same buildings, mountains, trees, etc., pass by again and again? So in the suburbs, you see the same strip-malls with the same fast-"food" joints, the same video stores, identical convenience marts, the same everything. There are endless housing subdivisions (whence the title of this song), which seem to be the product of some gigantic cookie cutter wielded by the hand of God. There are even upscale subdivisions with names like "Oak Tree Commons." One of these by itself might seem to have a certain charm, but then another row of them goes up a parking lot away, exactly the same, and you suddenly feel like a fly on a square of patterned wallpaper!

The city might have been dangerous, but at least (as Sartre could have told you) you knew you were alive. On the other hand, the suburbs have made a science of security to the point of making it a bath tank of body-temperature water. And don't think the suburban environment is a purely external one; it has seeped inside the skull. The same geometric order rigidly governs thought, behavior, and aspiration. The neural pathways of the brain are as tidy and well laid-out as the streets of Suburbia, USA, with as little room for eccentricity or unpredictability. Futures must follow paths as carefully preordained as bus routes. Growing up, we find that it all seems so one-sided. Opinions on every subject are all provided as in a catechism. The future is predecided, exactly as depicted in the movie *The Graduate*, where at his high school graduation party, the young Dustin Hoffman character is chilled to realize that having just exited what he thought to be the most regimented period of his life, he is about to be inducted into the ranks of two-dimensional, martini-drinking, golfball-chasing, country-clubbing professional drones. The watchword for a successful future: "Plastics."

It all seems so one-sided, because the side that is missing from the monologue of stifling suburban catechism is yours. If you were given any say in the matter, if all individuals were trusted to set their own courses, who knows what chaos (or what freedom) might result!? So your future is "Detached and subdivided," *i.e.*, detached from you, making your existence inauthentic, and subdivided; *i.e.*, the "geometric order" outside you is internalized so that you in turn can socialize and clip the wings of the next generation. Welcome to life in the mass-production zone. The link with "Grand Designs" is clear. The suburb is one of the labs, the matrices of the mass-production scheme.

"Subdivisions" might be profitably compared to another song about suburbia, the Monkees' "Pleasant Valley Sunday." There, too, we see a creepily convincing picture of suburban existence with its deadening torpor, like the delusive warmth felt by the advanced frostbite victim. The difference between the two songs is that "Pleasant Valley Sunday" implicitly depicts youth as rejecting the suburban lifestyle, while in "Subdivisions," there is the canny awareness that suburbanites are not created overnight, not kidnapped and brainwashed in some strategic puberty ritual. No, youth has its own conformism, a peer-pressure more ruthless and inflexible than even the Rotary Club orthodoxy of their parents. In the high school halls and in the shopping malls—in short, the two major gathering places of suburban youth—one must conform or be cast out. "Nerds," "wonks," "geeks," any kind of nonconformists, will feel the ostracism and ridicule once aimed by the crowd at the leper and the heretic.

The two images of the high school and the shopping mall are significant beyond their accurate depiction of the typical setting for teenage life. The two places are twin centers of propaganda instilling the conformer/consumer values of suburbia. In the high schools youth receives a homogenizing indoctrination into society's mores. It is certainly not education *per se* that Rush means to denigrate here, as witness the salute to science in "Countdown" later in the album, and the positive references to the mind and thinking throughout their work. No, we see the intention perfectly in the video for *Subdivisions*, in which the dreamer, the misfit is depicted as watching a Rush music video until irate parents shut off the set and toss a pile of school books at the lad. It is the anticonformist, pro-authenticity message "Subdivisions" preaches that suburbia's mass-production zone seeks to zone out with a particular kind of conventional value-education. This is the kind of "education" rejected by the youth who rise up in Pink Floyd's "The Wall" chanting that they don't need no education, no thought-control, *i.e.*, the kind of supposed education that is merely brainwashing, that inhibits rather than inspires thought. Rush's point is precisely the same as Paul Simon's: when he looked back on all the crap he learned in high school, he wondered how he could still think at all. The small-minded school marms who went into shrill hysterics on hearing lyrics like these only showed how perfectly they fit the stereotype of bad educators the songs condemn! Rather, all these songs were at least implicitly recommending what Neil Postman called *Teaching as a Subversive Activity*, the sort of teaching Socrates did: teaching how to *think for oneself.*

But it is not in a commercialistic society's interest to teach people to think. For if they did, how would the public continue to believe the unrelenting lies of advertisers? How would politicians be able to deceive the public with silly, feel-good campaign ads? How would fundamentalist TV preachers or dogma-dispensing churches control their flocks with superstitious threats of Hell?

If the high schools teach the values of a consumer/conformer society, the shopping malls are the "lab section" of the course. They are where you learn by doing, by buying. One sees drifting flocks of adolescents and teenagers attired in costumes so closely matched that they might as well be a troop of Boy Scouts, Girl Scouts, or even Hitler Youth! When all the girls have the same make-up, dress-styles, hairdos, earrings; all the boys wear the same shorts, caps, skateboards, T-shirts, aren't they really wearing uniforms? And as they wear them they drift from store to store, buying more and more. Youth in the mall is really a legion of recruits lining up at the recruitment station, enlisting in the army of Big Money. The sick joke is that they are fighting against themselves, yelling "Banzai!" to drive their true, authentic selves in disarray from the field.

If young people knew who the enemy was, things would suddenly look strikingly different. The commercials which try to sell you a soft drink because you are a member of the Pepsi Generation are utterly cynical. What on earth can make Pepsi more appropriate to an age group or a lifestyle than Coke, or A&P Cream Soda for that matter? It is cynical and manipulative conditioning, no different than B. F. Skinner's "operant conditioning," which manipulates a lab rat into associating two arbitrarily paired things: a green light and getting food. Every such commercial, pretending to promote your being cool, your entry into the in-crowd, ought to be recognized for the insidious propaganda it is. When Michael Jackson tells you to drink Pepsi so you'll be as cool as he is, you should recognize it as a latter-day counterpart to the old Nazi broadcasts in which the sultry voice of disc-jockey Axis Sally would try to persuade American soldiers to lay down their weapons and go home.

Of course youth likes to think it is rebellious. But the mass-production society doesn't mind certain forms of rebellion. They are harmless to it in the long-run. They only introduce habits, like alcohol and sex, that will become useful and profitable to the market-society later in life anyway. And, most important, these sham-rebellions, these "naughty" behaviors, are themselves mere exercises in conformity. In pine-panelled basement bars, in carseat lovenests, you prove yourself cool or you are cast out. Is it cool to get drunk? Should you have recreational sex because everybody's doing it? It is common to call such caving in to peer-pressure "lemming-like." The lemmings, of course, are supposed to rush *en masse* over the ledge to drown in the sea. Who would have guessed the simile would prove to be *literally* apt when teenage *suicide* actually became a fad a few years ago!

But the ominous emergence of that fatal fad underscores the truth of Rush's lyric. Any escape would be worth trying in order to forget momentarily the unattractive truth. Death, however, is not what Rush is getting at. The song goes on to talk about the escape many young people make into the city, reversing their parents' exodus. Since the suburbs lack any charms to soothe youth's restless dreams, youth hits the road for the very same city lights shunned by their elders. Doesn't this mean that "Subdivisions" does after all pose the same "generation-gap" opposition we find in "Pleasant Valley Sunday?" No, because the attentive listener soon discovers that for Rush, to exit the suburbs for the city is to jump out of the frying pan and into the fire. Note the image for the ageless, ancient attraction to the city: like moths drawn to the candle flame that will incinerate us, we drift haplessly into the city.

Once we walk through the doors of the Port Authority Terminal onto Eighth Avenue and up 42nd Street, we are mesmerized by the silently screaming neon lights. We take on a reflection of their glow, which yet somehow comes from an inner source. We feel what H. P.

Lovecraft called a sense of "adventurous expectancy," as we stride forth to become a part of it all. We want to check out all the flashing attractions. But we also want to *become* one of the glowing attractions. By our dress or make-up or manner we are lit up like fireflies, and our blinking radiance calls people to come check us out; we are cruising for the action. The night is alive like a jungle of bright shadows and we wish nothing so much as to become one with it.

The next lines seem to envision both possible extremes. Some will wind up selling their dreams for small desires. It is hard not to think here of New York's "Minnesota Strip," where young runaways to the City are quickly recruited as prostitutes. To survive in the big city, which rapidly turns out to be at least as formidable as it was fascinating, you may have to sink to turning tricks or selling drugs. So much for your dreams of making it in the metropolis.

But some do make it. Some succeed as professionals. Rush doesn't seem to envy their fate much either! These lose the race to faster rats. They find themselves caught in ticking traps, or in other words, they join the rat-race of high-pressure business. To join that race is to lose it, since it is a race to be first into the prison! The ticking trap is slavery to a schedule and to the punch-in time-clock, with the added inexorable doom of the ticking time-bomb.

And then you realize, once it begins to wear on you, that maybe your parents had a point in, some justification for, leaving the city. There's no turning back, at least not outwardly; but inwardly you begin to fantasize an escape from your escape! You start to dream of someplace where you might pause in your restless flight, somewhere that emerges out of a memory of lighted streets on quiet nights. Suburbia, that's where. Pretty ironic. Yet there is no suggestion you wouldn't do it the same way again!

The upshot is that suburbia *is* a place you'd need to escape from! But so is the city! But going around and around from one to the other, each successive generation switching places, is not the answer. There has to be an escape from *both* places to a Third. Where is *this* mysterious Shangri-La? A reference to it lurks unobtrusively at the end of the first stanza, waiting for you to notice it. Suburbia is an isolated quarter, a lonely no-man's land pitched between the bright lights and the far unlit unknown. This last is the third zone. On the literal level, this must refer to the countryside beyond the suburbs. But really the phrase evokes a more mysterious association than that. The far unlit unknown lies *within*. It is the authentic selfhood that has been suppressed and buried by the propaganda of both suburban and urban mass-production zones.

It is the much-neglected, seldom-visited *self-production* zone. It is the place where the dreamer or the misfit is not alone. Or rather is alone with himself, which may be the most enlightening and congenial company of all. In *this* unlit zone, what Jung called "the undiscovered self," we must reflect, contemplate, dialogue with the authentic self we had long since forgotten. And, fortunately, one may, though with difficulty, learn to live in this zone even though one lives outwardly in either suburbia or the city. This far unlit unknown can be the still point in the eye of the whirling storm of events and pressures. Dreams, a recurrent Rush theme, come to birth there, and we are nurtured. It is no coincidence that "Subdivisions" ends (*if* it ends—see below) with a busy clock-slave beginning to dream, beginning to journey to that zone of refuge.

"The Analog Kid"

But "Subdivisions" does not really end. The elipse (...) at the end of the last line obviously means "To be continued." And "Subdivisions" continues immediately with "The Analog Kid." This song may be read in two ways and probably should be read both ways. First, the idyllic scene of a young man daydreaming in the grass, his mind on far-off scenes of cities, forests, seas, and mountains, wishing to go there, is an enlarged cameo, a focused example of "Subdivi-sions"'s dreams of restless youth. Here is one such youth, dreaming such dreams in his young and restless heart, a clear wink referring you to the previous song. The city is at least one of the dream sirens which call out, enticing him, just as "Subdivisions." "Analog Kid"'s references to buildings with eyes (*i.e.*, the lit windows in the buildings) and to city lights and busy streets hark back to "Subdivisions," too. In "Subdivisions" we heard of the timeless old attraction of the city, and even so in "The Analog Kid," the dreamer responds to the vision of the city which calls him again and again.

A sun-tanned maiden, perhaps a wood-nymph, dances in his dreams, and her voice is redolent of the mythic music of the spheres. The boy may dream of romance, but that is not precisely what this lovely vision portends. She is a faun or nymph from classical mythology. She represents the enchantment of dream, the alluring siren-call of the wide world. The music of the spheres is another image for the same thing. Eccentric astronomer Johannes Kepler, to whom we owe the Laws of Planetary Motion, thought he could hear the heavenly sounds made by the planetary spheres as they sail gracefully through the void. No NASA radio telescope has ever picked up that music, but dreamers continue to hear it. Really what The Analog Kid is hearing is what Walt Whitman called *A Song of Myself*, the self he could be if he listened to his dreams.

It is a self that could soar through the skies. For a moment the boy imagines he sees that self aloft on the wings of dream—but then the nymph's voice is dispelled with the more mundane tones of his mother calling him to supper, or to do his homework, and he realizes that the soaring form was but a hawk.

The young dreamer pulls down his baseball cap over his eyes. Like the humanoid escapee in "The Body Electric," he is experiencing overload, a clash of signals, a confusion of programming. Whose voice will he heed? That of the dryad or of his mother? Heartstrings, or apron-strings? He will leave home; there is really no question about that, but when? And what will the change mean? When he leaves he won't know what he's hoping to find. When he leaves he won't know what he's leaving behind. Another elipse; this song does not end either. Where does it lead? Forward to "Digital Man" and backward to "Subdivisions." Yes, back to the previous song, because "Analog Kid" is not simply a specific case of "Subdivisions"'s restless dreams of youth. It is also a specific example of a dream of somewhere to relax, somewhere out of a memory. The rat-race runner, the time-clock prisoner of "Subdivisions" seeks refuge in the memory of the old days when as a youth he lay in the meadow dreaming of a future full of promising horizons and of dangerous blind alleys. Having been trapped in one of the latter, the rat-race-runner (the Digital Man, as we will soon see) thinks back to the moment when he paused at the crossroads. Now, by contrast, he knows rather too well what he has left behind.

"Digital Man"

The title character in "Digital Man" is he who left behind his identity as the Analog Kid. The Digital Man is the creature of a world of high-speed technology, of the breakneck pace, of a rat-race in which human beings sooner or later wear down and burn out because they are forced to try to match the pace of tireless, instant-replay machines. "Digital Man" is pretty much the same image as the humanoid, the android, the machine-man with plastic skin and an electric body. Only here the focus is less on his denatured degradation as it is on his function as a cog in a wheel, a living computer chip, already depersonalized and soon to be discarded.

"Digital Man" is connected by clear clues to "The Analog Kid" before it and to "New World Man" after it. The titles make this clear, even though "Digital Man" is separated on either side by another song. "Chemistry," a song about interpersonal relationships, similar in theme to "Entre Nous," does not quite fit into the sequence between "The Analog Kid," and "Digital Man," but this is not just because of its content. Notice, if you will, that "Chemistry" is one of the few songs co-written by Geddy Lee and Alex Lifeson with Neil Peart. The other songs in the sequence are all the work of Peart alone. "Chemistry," then, is foreign matter, an interpolation, put there as an interlude between the segments of the sequence.

The same goes for "The Weapon," which has been placed between "Digital Man" and "New World Man." What is it doing here? Of course "The Weapon" is an intruder from yet another sequence, the

Fear Trilogy, as the subtitle tells you. To interpose "The Weapon" in this manner, right in the middle of "Digital Man" and "New World Man," serves notice that the two sequences ("Subdivisions" + "The Analog Kid" + "Digital Man" + "New World Man" and the Fear Trilogy) interlock in meaning. They are explorations of aspects of the same phenomenon, as you can see by comparing the present chapter with the previous one.

As to the titles, the "Digital Man" is "The Analog Kid" grown up, having left his idyllic meadow (or his suburban park) to go into the big city. The sequence is plain both from the ordering of the songs and from the titles. They reflect the graduation of the recording industry from analogue recording, in which magnetic tape picks up a sine wave and produces an approximate copy of the master, to digital recording (Compact Discs and Digital Audio Tape), in which a computer records innumerable tiny bytes of sound, resulting in a more faithful reproduction, another original. Why use these terms for the child and the adult? Because this particular individual exists nowhere but on Rush's album. This purely literary character is a bit of recording (though he may symbolize you and me).

"Digital Man" carries echoes of anthropological categories, of Neanderthal Man as opposed to the later Cro-Magnon Man. Even so, Digital Man evolves into, or gives way to, New World Man, a new and superior breed to whom we will turn our attention later. While the New World Man will take control of the system and remake it in his image, the Digital Man is himself merely a component in the system.

Attuned to the breakneck pace of the electronic world, he lives with the breathless haste of a light-impulse traveling over an optical circuit in a phone line. Like the spreading energy signal itself, he only picks up scraps of information from the radio, radiation from the dancers and romancers who seem to have the answers, but really possess no clue. He lives (we live) in the age of the information revolution. Information is everywhere, and the goal is to transmit ever more of it, not to evaluate it, never to ask the old question of truth. One need ask no such questions (advertisers and politicians do not), since it is utterly irrelevant to communication, persuasion, gaining an end. And with no awareness of the truth (or that there is such a thing), how can there be so much as a "clue" to the *meaning* of life? Meaning depends on truth. Both become unguessable fantasies in an age of mere information.

In many ways, the perfect example of a Digital Man might be Winston Smith, the hapless anti-hero of George Orwell's nightmare masterpiece, *Nineteen Eighty-Four*. Smith is a card-carrying member of the Party, the ruling clique of Oceania, an imaginary totalitarian state. He works in the Ministry of Truth, but in the deceptive language of Oceania, "Newspeak," Truth is mutable, infinitely malleable. It works this way: the past is changeable, since at any given time the past exists only as *memory* and *record*. If by intimidation a government can alter memory, and if by careful rewriting and censoring the authorities can change the record, they will effectively have changed the past, the only past there is to know. Our task is to believe faithfully in the *latest version* of the past and to give no credence to previous versions—*which no longer exist!*

So our man Smith, low-level Party functionary, is busy daily at his desk, industriously turning history into propaganda, censoring and counterfeiting newspapers according to official dictates. He controls the information to be fed to the masses. Yet he himself scarcely escapes the scrutiny of his shadowy superiors. A two-way TV screen in his tiny apartment keeps him under constant surveillance. In the course of the book he tries to live a covert life, but he is inevitably found out. His world is under constant, omnicient, always monitored, observation. This is beginning to sound like a musical version of *Nineteen Eighty-Four!* Winston Smith, the Digital Man, is simply a part of the telescope through which Big Brother spies on us and Smith alike.

But in at least one respect Smith is unlike the Digital Man. He is not a victim of what Marx called "false consciousness." It is Smith's Hell to perceive with acuity just where he fits into the scheme of things. By contrast, the Digital Man has become so wholly a part of the mechanism that he perceives no incongruity. He has not reached the humanoid escapee's point of self-revelation. He does not hear the call of his buried human nature. He has tuned it out. Like the mentally vacuous gardener-cum-presidential candidate Chance in Jerzy Kosinski's *Being There*, the Digital Man's reality is to float in a sea of rapidly switching channels, video scenes with neither context nor continuity, and so with no possible meaning. A recollection of his selfhood, should it surface momentarily, could scarcely be noticed, wedged in knife-edged as it must be between split-second images and sound-bites. The collector of information scraps is quite adept at adaptation. He has to be, because, for strangers and arrangers like himself, constant change is here to stay. Digital Man is Change; Digital Man is Chance.

Digital Man is the living embodiment of the Buddhist doctrine of *kshanika*, "flux." Why is there suffering in the world, and seemingly nothing but suffering? Buddhists say it is because fulfillment is an illusory now-moment between the ache of frustration and the sorrow of disappointment or boredom. Our problem is that we seek satisfaction, *i.e.*, something immovable, a rock of security amid a world that is nothing but constant change. No wonder there is no fulfillment to be found in the world! But if it sounds strange to you that life is suffering, because you are pretty happy with it, it shows that you have completely adjusted to the flux. The fleeting will-o'-the-wisp *change* is itself your goal! You seek nothing more lasting than the momentary. This is why man is adept at adaptation: constant change is here to stay. But this is to embrace existence as a phantom. It is unreal, insubstantial, *inauthentic* existence.

But inauthentic existence, as we have seen, is just the kind that *succeeds* in the mass-production zone. It is being "well-adjusted" to a *sick society!* Nonetheless, Digital Man will be lionized as was Chance in *Being There.* As a living video void, Chance was the perfect hero for a TV-reared society. He was a blank screen on which everyone's images might be projected. Ronald Reagan was in some ways a real-life Chance, a great President because he was a "Great Communicator." A Digital Man for our time. Like Reagan and like Chance, Rush's "Digital Man" has a date with destiny in a black sedan; he will ride with the great in their limousines, the just spoils of the system to which he has obediently conformed.

The great plague of the professional class in our day is surely not conscience pangs, but rather *stress.* This is the only signal that manages to penetrate in any measure to tell the Digital Man that he is betraying his true nature. He is not a machine, though he has been lulled into thinking that he is. In some ways it's easier that way. His life is lived benumbed, under anaesthetic. It is neatly subdivided: robotic and synthetic. (Subdivided! This adult world is the logical fruition of the conformity-training of adolescence in the suburbs we saw in "Subdivisions.") Like an athlete whose sprains and wounds are cruelly deadened, but not cared for, so he can finish the game, with no thought for post-game health, the Digital Man plays in the fast-forward mode as long as he can stand it, burning the candle at both ends, until "burn-out" claims another victim. And then a Club Med vacation ought to patch him up.

If being occasionally "stressed out" is the only tap on the shoulder the Digital Man will allow to remind him all is not right, his daydreams of escape are his only near-recognition of his true nature—that he is born to better things, destined for better realms. He'd just love to spend the night in Zion because he's been a long while in Babylon. Like the sixth century B.C. Jews, deported to a half-century exile in a foreign land (Babylon), the Digital Man dimly recollects that he, too, once lived in a Promised Land (Zion), and that this is not it! What he'd really like is a pair of wings with which to soar off to the tropic isle of Avalon. Avalon is where King Arthur waits to return to England's aid in her darkest hour. But it is too late for the Digital Man. King Arthur, Digital Man's authentic self, asleep far away, will now never come back. Because Digital Man no longer realizes he is in peril and thus will never summon him.

Digital Man as a species may still be ascendant, but his fate is sealed. The mechanical world of which he is a part must eventually collapse under its own weight. The human spirit will burst forth like the Phoenix from its own pyre, and in that day we will see the emergence of the New World Man. And in the meantime, Rush calls any

Digital Men and Women who may be listening to make the change now. Become such a man or woman and so hasten the coming of the New World.

"Tom Sawyer"

Having come to the brink of "New World Man," we are going to hold off discussing it till Chapter IV, "Castles in the Distance," because the political elements of the song will make most sense in the context of songs like "Natural Science," "Territories," and "Farewell to Kings." Meantime, we choose to spotlight "Tom Sawyer" as the logical fruition of the train of thought we have been following through the previous songs. It is clear that Tom Sawyer and New World Man are the same character, the same ideal, and "Tom Sawyer" may actually be a clearer statement about personal authenticity, a more natural alternative and sequel to "Grand Designs," "The Body Electric," "Subdivisions," "The Analog Kid," and "Digital Man."

"Tom Sawyer" has become the anthem of Rush, because Rush fans clearly discern in it the central vision of the group, the essence of the gospel Rush preaches. It is a sketch of a modern-day warrior, and the implied message is *recruitment*. Picture the U.S. Marine Corps poster, "The Marines are looking for a few good men." So is Rush. Will you join the corps? Become "today's Tom Sawyer"?

Whence Tom Sawyer's mean pride? Why does he enter with such a mean stride? Don't put down his proud swagger to mere arrogance. Chalk it up rather to *inner-directedness*. Here is someone who has not sought (or, like the humanoid, has escaped from) shelter under the gun. His beliefs and decisions are his own, right or wrong, not programmed by the masters of the mass-production zone. His allegiance is not available for lease to any religious or political cause that he has not created himself. Renting out one's mind implies not just an *abdication*, but a handing over of the mind to others for some *return*. One who "rents" his mind, not just "surrenders" it, is making a trade; he gets shelter and security, the anesthetic comfort of no longer having to trouble his head to think for himself and live with his decisions.

But today's Tom Sawyer isn't playing that game. Here is someone, anyone, with *authenticity*. Leaving himself vulnerable to pain and error, he is at the same time open to acute joys, profound thrills of which the programmed android, the mass-produced Digital Man, will know nothing.

If one shuts off the senses so as to escape pain, it works both ways, and pleasure will be ruled out, too. By contrast, Tom Sawyer feels with exquisite clarity. The world is deep; the world is deep. Love and life are deep. These thoughts echo Friedrich Nietzsche's: "The world is deep, and deeper than the day could read. Deep is its woe. Joy deeper still than grief can be. Woe says: Hence, go! But

45

joys want all eternity, want deep, profound eternity." In various works, Nietzsche preached a philosophy of joy, of will, of the prerogative of the "superman" (Colin Wilson's "Outsider") to seize the day. It is his right to create new and bold values, to wrest the sceptre from the infirm, palsied, and withered hands of those who have ruled the world with timidity, with fear and hatred of life and of its vivid joys. "Tom Sawyer" is Rush's image of the superman, Nietzsche's Prophet Zarathustra. Because he has the boldness to seize it, the future is his. His eyes are as wide as the world is deep. His horizons are unlimited, his skies as wide as love and life are deep. The world is within his grasp because his grasp is wide enough to encompass it. This is why what you say about his company mirrors what you say about society—he represents the wave of the future. He is the New World Man.

A more explicit literary clue to our hero's character is, of course, Mark Twain's *The Adventures of Tom Sawyer*. Why should Peart have chosen this name? What is it about Twain's Missouri mischief-maker that makes him a fit analogue for Rush's New World role-model? If we had to characterize Twain's Tom Sawyer, to sum up what it is about him that makes him do what he does, we might sum him up this way. Tom Sawyer is someone who manages to see through the entrenched silliness of the adult world around him, not because he has learned to see through it the hard way, gradually becoming disillusioned through bitter disappointment; nor because he enters it from outside and sees candidly with undimmed eyes that the Emperor wears no clothes; but rather because, like a social mutant, he is born equipped with canniness and craftiness. The usual tricks don't fool him; he is too clever for them. Thus armed, Tom Sawyer avoids being manipulated by the late-Victorian, provincial-American society into which he is born, even though he must sometimes pay a high price for it. In turn, his gifts enable him to manipulate the system (and his contemporaries).

With his cleverness comes courage. He can stand up to Injun Joe as well as outwit Aunt Polly. Another ingredient is a certain youthful *naïveté*. His clear vision of the absurdity of what surrounds him does not always extend to the absurdity of his own hopes, and he may make several false starts, yet none of these finally discourages him. He remains always hopeful, yet discontent.

Tom Sawyer is not the only Mark Twain character in this song. Anonymous but present is Tom's pal Huckleberry Finn. Surely it is Huck's raft on which our hero is riding out the river of the day's events. In *The Adventures of Huckleberry Finn*, Huck is another "noble savage" who must piece together the confused fragments of the adult world. A system self-evident to parents, Sunday School teachers, and slaveholders is utter mystery to Huck. He learns of these mysteries, though never able to accept them, as he rides the tides of the Mississippi with the runaway slave Jim. The river is a classic image of life and its vicissitudes. It functions the same way, for instance, in Hermann Hesse's *Siddhartha*.

It is the riding on the river that sets apart Tom Sawyer from his opposite number, the Digital Man. Life is a river of ceaseless change. That fact, paradoxically, will not change: He knows that particular changes aren't permanent, but the phenomenon of change is. Digital Man knows it, too, but he has elected to become part of it, a piece of debris tossed about amid the storm of flux. As a result he has no abiding character. But Tom Sawyer has found a way to keep the tides of change from engulfing him. Rather than surrendering to them, he surfs along on their crest. True, he cannot help moving, but as he does so, he maintains a stable identity, his integrity. He remains himself *inside*, where it matters. Hence "his reserve," his hanging back from the invitations to join this or that cause or to submerge himself (like Eric Hoffer's *True Believer)* into some mass-movement. It is a real, though a quiet, defense.

To remain afloat *atop* the swirling flood allows at least the possibility of steering one's own course. This becomes impossible as soon as one is immersed in it; then one is doomed, like Digital Man, to be swept along aimlessly until one crashes somewhere along the banks. Tom Sawyer does not hold himself aloof, despite his reserve, his defense, his rising above it all. He has charted his course forward into history. He will not sit out the struggle. He plunges right into the friction of the day. After all, what good is a warrior without a battle?

III.

IN TOUCH WITH SOME REALITY

"Time Stand Still" and "Turn the Page"

"Digital Man" and the songs related to it draw a depressing picture of the flux-existence of our time, a fast-paced whirlpool that sucks us down before we know it. "Tom Sawyer" represents the resourceful person who realizes the danger and is able at least to ride the current and sometimes able to swim against it. In this chapter we will take a look at a related theme: change as an inevitable condition for life, the medium in which we swim like fish. We fear it like a person waving his arms to regain balance and avoid falling off a pier into a lake, but it may be that if we approached it with the right preparation, a mask and an aqualung, we might find an unsuspected world of beauty there.

Appropriately, in view of the subject matter, "Time Stand Still" (*Hold Your Fire*, 1987) opens not with a thought or a theory, but with the first-person recollection of a razor thin "now-moment," a split-second pause to collect your thoughts before you resume your driven, head-long plunge down the currents of the time-stream. This is, of course, a song, specifically a lament, about *change*. We find a similar montage of images in "Turn the Page," another song from the same album: a time capsule; white-water rafting down the time-stream; someone adrift in a wind tunnel, buffeted by the gusts of future-shock.

The theme of these songs recalls that of "Tom Sawyer": no changes are permanent, but change is. This insight is by no means new; many great thinkers have pondered the phenomenon of change and what it implies about life, the world, and human existence. Rush, too, is concerned with these broader dimensions of change. Songs like "Digital Man" and "Tom Sawyer" consider the questions of human identity and integrity as functions of the change process and how one reacts to it. Will you ride atop the surging wave and so maintain an identity distinct from it? Today's Tom Sawyer does. Or will you become a bobbing cork carried mindlessly with the flood tide? Digital Man does that.

But "Time Stand Still" and "Turn the Page" raise a somewhat different set of questions, more metaphysical ones. The implied answers are sometimes rather vague because of the evocative, non-analytical medium of poetry.

They may, however, take on more distinct form if we try to view them against the background of two carefully elaborated theories of change. These are the philosophy of Heraclitus and the mysticism of Gotama Buddha, both of whom evolved their philosophies of change in the sixth century B.C., within a few decades of each other, yet many thousands of miles apart. Heraclitus lived in Ephesus of Asia Minor, Gotama in Nepal and India.

Heraclitus put his philosophy succinctly in a striking and memorable sentence: "One cannot step into the same river twice." The idea is that there is no static *thing* called a river. It is simply a *channel of change*, a name for a continuous process of replacement of water by more water, and that by still more. Whereas this condition of change is obvious in the case of a river, Heraclitus's point was that the river is not an exception to the rule: it *is* the rule. Though it is less obvious to us, even the mountains are *constantly* changing and eroding. Species are evolving. Why do we not see it? Simply because we are creatures of a moment. As the Bible says, we are like grass, flourishing today, tomorrow thrown into a fire for kindling. We live such brief and frenetic lives that our attention spans are adjusted to them, and we can only see changes that change even faster than we do! But all things change. Heraclitus's disciple Cratylus put the same point even more acutely: "One cannot step into the same river once." There is, strictly speaking, no river. To call it by a name implies a continuous, stable identity that nothing has! Rather than saying "There is no river," it might be better to say "No river is." Rather, all rivers (all things) are *becoming*.

Change, then, is the only constant. No changes are permanent, but change is. Yet if there is no *permanence*, there is at least *regularity*, as the old cliché (quoted by Rush in "Circumstances") has it, "The more things change, the more they stay the same." The world, though ablaze with constant change, is not surreal in its randomness. Things always seem to change along certain paths and in certain patterns. For instance, when you heat water, once it gets to a certain temperature, it always boils, it doesn't sometimes *freeze*. It doesn't turn into orange juice. Perhaps it is true, as Rush sings in "Prime Mover," that anything can happen, but we do not see all manner of arbitrary, unpredictable changes. We see melting watches only in Salvador Dali's paintings.

Similarly, there is a regular *proportion* in change. Though water can become steam and ice, and back and forth, and such changes are always happening, the proportions of water, ice, and steam are always pretty constant. It's never 90 percent ice at the same time. Though Heraclitus couldn't have known it, the Law of Conservation of Matter and Energy is a beautiful illustration of his theory. What accounts for this stability in a world of flux? The Logos, or divine reason, orders all things, Heraclitus decided. Some centuries later Xeno of Citium would build on these insights and use them to create the philosophy and ethics of Stoicism. We will take a closer look at Stoicism when we come to consider "Limelight."

Gotama Buddha would have agreed with most of what Heraclitus and Cratylus said, though he would have stopped short of explaining the regularity of change. The Buddha was skeptical of pure philosophical speculation because he had seen it used too often to distract attention from solving the far more pressing problems of human existence. But like his Greek counterpart, he observed that all about us we see naught but constant change. And in this fact he decided he had found the reason for human sorrow and despair. Why does it seem we never find real satisfaction in this world? We do not find it because we *cannot* find it in a world like ours. And that is because it is simply not here to be found!

Put it this way: what would satisfaction mean? Wouldn't it mean you have at last found what you can be content with? A career achievement, a relationship, an amount of money? You can henceforth rest in static bliss, one long sigh of relief, right? Alas, observed the Buddha, you cannot find any port of rest in the storm of constant change! *Everything* changes, nothing stays still, stays the same, long enough for you to rest satisfied with it. It will change, or you will, or circumstances will change. Youth and beauty will fade, the ardor of love will cool, money will run out. And then you will be back on the road, searching for some new Grail to give you "satisfaction" again. Mick Jagger couldn't seem to get any satisfaction. The Buddha could have told him why. No port in the storm of change. This changing world of frustration and disappointment the Buddha called *Samsara*.

Later Buddhist theoreticians coined two technical terms to sum up the doctrine of change and its implications. First, *kshanika*, or "flux," describes the situation: all is ceaselessly in process. Second, anicca, "impermanence," describes the nature of things in light of *kshanika*. That is, you are not some changeless quantity being carried along by the surging waves of change but otherwise immune to them. No, you yourself, like all things, *are* in the process of changing. As only a few years pass, little is the same about you except your DNA. Everything else will have changed: your height, weight, maybe your hair color and style, your opinions and interests, even your name if you don't like it.

Still later Buddhist thinkers reasoned that if nothing abides, if nothing is "the same" for two instants in a row, then nothing can be said to have any subsisting nature, any substance, any *reality*. Things have "no *dharmas*." *Dharma* means "law," and laws supposedly describe or dictate abiding conditions: things are or should be always such-and-such a way. But "always" is an illusion. Things are not constant enough to enable us to speak of the laws of their being, in other words of their *nature,* their *reality.* (Or, as Faust says to Mephistopheles, "By changing floods the world itself is broken, / Yet you'll invent a little pledge to bind me?")

Rush puts the idea well in "Turn the Page": truth is a swiftly moving target that you can't quite fix in the cross-hairs. No one is a good enough marksman to bag it. So how, pray tell, can anybody be enlightened? Not by mastering some "unchanging truth," that's for sure, for there is no unchanging truth. But maybe there is a different kind of enlightenment.

Just as in Buddhism, the beginning of enlightenment is to realize the truth of flux and impermanence. Don't continue to seek the permanent where it cannot be found. This lesson occurs in the refrain of "Turn the Page." At first glance these lines might seem to mean that the crazy, hectic pace to which we all are nowadays subject is just an unfortunate byproduct of the particular age we live in, that this age is but a stage that will be over sooner or later, so in the meantime why not make the best of it?

But perhaps this is too superficial a reading. Rather, might we not see the age in question as being a long time that will seemingly never end, as implied in the phrase "the age we live in," which means to say we cannot escape it and choose another age we might prefer to live in instead? Yet in the next line, the seemingly changeless age is relativized: it's just a stage—despite your timebound worm's eye view, even an age, an epoch, an eon, is transient. "This, too, shall pass." So do not either despair or be falsely content. Disengage yourself from the age. Here in fact is the Buddha's prescription for escaping the insidious treadmill of Samsara: stop *desiring* it. Realize it is a *dead end.* According to Buddhist doctrine, you continue to be reincarnated in this world because you never learn your lesson, that you're barking up the wrong tree, that satisfaction is not to be found in Samsara, but only in *Nirvana,* an unimaginable state of consciousness where the fire of craving is extinguished. As long as you remain unenlightened on this point, you are locked into what Buddhists call the Twelvefold Chain of Causation. Suffice it to say this is a vicious cycle of escaping from a life of frustration at death only to plunge right back into the same no-win race in another incarnation. To attain Nirvana, you need to disengage from the chain of causation.

Early Buddhists seem to have believed that to renounce the world of Samsara you had to turn your back on society and human life, become a monk, a nun, a hermit. But later Buddhists came to believe that the enlightened person would be able still to navigate in the world of Samsara but, thanks to his enlightened perspective, he should be able to see Nirvana *within* Samsara. It's all in your viewpoint. Yes, changeable worldly things are not the answer. They may not even be particularly *real.* But neither are they to be despised. Experience Sam-

saric reality in such a way as not to take it for more than it is, and you
will be fine. Zen meditation in particular is aimed at transforming consciousness so as to see eternity in a moment of time, peace in a second
of turmoil, the One behind the many fragments.

It is exactly such an enlightened person who is mentioned in
"Time Stand Still": one who would like to pause like some pilgrim
learning to transcend, to live as if each step were the last. According to
Zen Buddhism, each moment is as the last (or the first) because each
has its own integrity. You see and do what you see and do in that moment, regardless of how things may have been different a moment before, or may be different a moment from now. One Zen anecdote tells
of a monk who is chased to a cliff edge by a tiger. He falls over and
manages to break his fall by grasping a slender sapling growing out of
the cliff face. But the roots begin to break, one by one, under his
weight. The monk's thoughts in that moment, perhaps his last on
earth? He notices a blossom on the sapling and savors its beauty. The
moment in which he encounters the beauty of the blossom is the only
moment in existence just then. Soon it will change, but for *this* moment, the only one you've ever got, the Zen advice is "Be here now."
And be fully present in, fully present to, the *next* moment when it
comes, too. Only so can you catch a glimpse of Nirvana in Samsara.

The result is a dazzling combination of belief in the value of
each moment and a full realization of the fleeting transience of all
things. The Buddhist philosopher-mystic Nagarjuna worked this out in
its most elaborate form. We call it Nagarjuna's dialectic, and it will
repay careful study if you are interested.

But our job here is to discuss some Rush songs. In this one we
have an intimation of Nagarjuna's dialectic. Life is like a novel. You
find it so intriguing that you just can't put it down. In the simple activity of reading an enjoyable book a paradox is implicit. If you enjoy
the book, you are eager to finish it, since you are swept up in it and
can't wait to see what finally happens. Yet precisely because you enjoy
the book you almost don't *want* to finish it! You wish it wouldn't end!
But of course it wouldn't be enjoyable if it didn't end, because there
would then be no plot, no dramatic tension, no narrative pace. If you
really appreciate the book for what it is, you will *savor it but finish it.*
You will keep turning the pages. And if you have grasped Nagarjuna's
dialectic, you will be more satisfied than disappointed when you are
done. Not expecting that the book might be endless, not believing there
will come no other good books, you will be happy to have enjoyed this
book, not bitterly rueful that *the* book is now done. In such terms we
should see life: it is to be enjoyed for what it is (beautiful but
ephemeral), not mourned for what it is not (eternally satisfying). Living so will prepare one for Nirvana when this life is over, for one will
know better than to seek to come back for the same thrill, better than to
turn back to the first page as soon as you finish the last one.

Hence the attitude we feel in "Time Stand Still." The point is not to look back, only to take a more careful, lingering look at one's present surroundings, the people and the places, *right now*. Because before you know it, experience slips away. In other words, "be here now," be fully aware of that blossom now, while it is and you are, because only in such moments, fully embraced, fully experienced, can you participate for a moment in that eternity (*Sunyata*, the Void) that lies implicit in all fleeting things.

To freeze the present moment a little longer means that the singer wants to have the leisure to see it fully before it passes, but freezing the moment is a figure of speech. It is really *perception*, not the moment itself, that must change. It is the difference between the Digital Man and Tom Sawyer that the first is lost in the storm of change, while the second has become a pilgrim who has learned to transcend. He knows good and well that no changes are permanent, but change is, yet he is able to keep a perspective above change.

It is, finally, significant that the apostrophic prayer for time to stand still really means just to slow down change or, as we have just seen, to focus more sharply our perception of it. It is a long-standing theme of Rush that we cannot escape flux and decay by calling a total halt to change. If we could, it would only be *instant* death, not *gradual* death! Some choice! To see this, compare the title refrain with Faust's words to Mephistopheles, who has purchased his soul with the promise of an endless series of pleasures and thrills. Faust says, "If to the fleeting hour I say / 'Remain, so fair thou art, remain!' / Then bind me with your fatal chain, / For I will perish in that day." (Goethe's *Faust*). Beauty and joy cannot be stopped in their tracks. They exist only as living things. Frozen, abstracted, they are destroyed.

The same insight forms the basis of the song "Xanadu" (*Farewell to Kings*, 1977). There, a quester after immortality, *i.e.*, freedom from change and decay, finds it in the icy caves of Xanadu, only to discover that eternity means frozen changelessness, paralysis. If all is change, even death is inevitable, but just as surely life is found nowhere else but in the timestream. For even when we transcend it we do not escape it.

We have seen that one of Rush's recurrent themes is the fact of change and the choice of one's reaction to it. In "Time Stand Still" and "Turn the Page" we examined insights suggesting the Buddhist doctrines of flux (*kshanika*) and impermanence (*anicca*), and how, like their Buddhist parallels, Rush's ideas on universal change imply a certain lack of reality in things (no *dharmas*, *Sunyata*, emptiness). When we turn to "Limelight" and "The Camera Eye" we find the unreality of the world set forth from a different angle, using a different metaphor: that of the performing stage. This potent image, as suggestive of varying associations as a Rorschach ink blot test, has yielded several theories about life and its not-quite-real quality, and we will see that certain allusions in the cryptic lyrics of "Limelight" reflect a number of these theories. The song is one of the most thought-provoking in the Rush canon.

"Limelight"

On the most obvious level, "Limelight" seems to be concerned with the emptiness of show business, an existence which many non-performers, at least nonprofessionals, envy. To these strivings and dreams, Rush at first seems to be saying, "Save yourselves the trouble, kids—it's not worth it; we're in a position to know. You're better off without all the dishonesty and compromise. Get on with real life instead." And this certainly is part of "Limelight"'s message. In fact, let's jump down to the fifth stanza to explore this aspect of the song. Rush hasn't the heart to lie; they can't pretend a stranger is a lifelong friend. The reference here is surely to the nauseatingly sleazy showbiz convention of schmaltzy pseudo-sentimentality. It's never been parodied better than on SCTV's *Sammy Maudlin Show*, where the garishly-sequined guests Bobby Bitman and Lola Heatherton gushingly emote all over each other, and host Sammy praises their Vegas routines and night club gigs in inflated terms verging on worship. In the loathsome mutual admiration society that is show business, air-headed stars are always "loving" each other, proclaiming each other as "terrific people," great friends, even if, as one suspects, they've never met until two minutes before the curtain rises. This is slimelight as much as limelight, and Rush wants no part of it. It is an issue of integrity. Why does the singer "have no heart to lie" in such circumstances? Precisely because, as the immediately preceding lines remind him, whatever he does, he will be doing it for all eyes to see. On the stage, before the cameras, one makes one's stand. You are living your life in the fisheye lens of the *paparazzi*, caught like a bug under a microscope within the unblinking camera eye. Do you really want to be seen by all eyes making a hypocrite of yourself?

Strangely, given human psychology, that is precisely the *first* thing most of us think to do! The power and humor of *Candid Camera* was always that someone's "real you" was being revealed, exposed— because they *did not know* they were being watched! Had they known, they'd have acted cooler, less spontaneous, less honestly and authentically, and that's what they later wish they *could* have done: "saved face," albeit a false front. But really, how much worse to be caught by the camera playing the hypocrite! Immortalized on celluloid as a liar, a phony. Better to look foolish, come to think of it, than to be a hypocrite. Other hypocrites will applaud you, but what has happened to your integrity? It vanished, melted away under the heat of the stage lights along with your self. If you play the slick phony for public acclaim, you have decided to identify with a superficial appearance rather than underlying reality, and whatever you do decide to identify yourself with *becomes* your self. If you identify with superficiality, the resulting you is a superficial one with no depth.

The phoniness of showbiz is a pandemic plague in our society. By comparison with the stars whose exploits they view on screen, many common Americans regard their own lives as pitiful nothings. So they live vicariously through their Hollywood or MTV idols. They gossip over lunch about the marital or financial troubles of the stars as if they were their own personal friends, which they wish they were! What pathetic delusion! Here is a flight from mundane reality to take refuge on the lighted stage, or at least to fancy that you bask in the spillover glow of the footlights. How far is this kind of delusion from the craziness of nonentity Rupert Pupkin in *The King of Comedy*, who convinced himself and others that he was a friend of a TV star? The readers of supermarket tabloids and viewers of *Entertainment Tonight* have come almost as close, pretending as they do that a stranger is a lifelong friend.

But the phoniness runs in the other direction, too. Have you ever wondered why the checkout-line papers fabricate soap-operatic stories about the most popular celebrities? What they are doing is to create a second level of fictional entertainment to satisfy the celebrities' fans. Cosby fans could not seem to get enough of his antics on TV, even with nightly syndicated reruns, so to meet the demand, the tabloids created a Cosby soap opera, making up "news" about backstage squabbles or about *Cosby* cast-members' imaginary divorces or bastard children or drug-busts. This was a *second* Cosby show. It is not as if the celebrities themselves do not aid and abet the process. The simple practice of coining stage names is already the creation of a second level of fiction, like Kal-el, whose pseudonym is Clark Kent, whose pseudonym is Superman. Infinite regress, with the *selves* of both star and fan receding into the media mist.

Vicarious identification with showbiz icons, then, is a way of retreating from one's own real world. And realizing this we have reached a second important theme in "Limelight." The song not only condemns the phoniness of the world of media; it also attacks the dreams of those who wish they could live in that world because reality is not good enough for them. Living in the limelight is the universal dream of all those who wish to *seem*, and *only* to seem: those who wish to escape any authentic existence as the selves their untapped abilities and untried opportunities would make them. By contrast, those who wish to *be* something must put aside the alienation from the real world facing them. They must get on with the fascinating business of life, the genuine relatedness to what life is really, beneath it all, about. They would find real life much more of a fascinating adventure if they dared *live* it. The *real* relation is that in which they stand to the world of people and tasks around them. Rush is speaking to people like the singer-character in Blondie's song "The Real World," who shouts defiantly (and solipsistically!) that she's not living in the real world no more, no more, no more!

What is the underlying theme? Why, the theme of the play of life, of course. And here "Limelight" begins to connect with an important philosophical view of the world as a play on stage, the view of Stoicism. The second-century AD Roman emperor Marcus Aurelius was one of the great Stoics. He bequeathed us his thoughts in a short book called *The Meditations.* In it he twice compares life to a theatrical performance. "An empty pageant; a stage play..., puppets, jerking on their strings—that is life. In the midst of it all you must take your stand, good-temperedly and without disdain, yet always aware that a man's worth is no greater than the worth of his ambitions" (7:3). "Reflect often how all the life of today is a repetition of the past; and observe that it also presages what is to come. Review the many complete dramas and their settings, all so similar, which you have known in your own experience, or from bygone history.... The performance is always the same; it is only the actors who change" (10:27).

As a Stoic, Marcus Aurelius believed that life was like a theater performance primarily because *it has a script,* an underlying theme. It is not random behavior, no matter how much it may appear that way to the audience. Imagine, however, that the actors on stage were unaware that they had any lines! What pointless chaos would result! Many people live needlessly troubled lives, the Stoics held, because they never learn about, or choose to disregard, the script. Zeus (read: God) wrote the "script" for human existence in that he created and controls all things by his Logos, or divine reason. All that happens to you has a purpose and is aimed at improving your character if you will but receive it in that positive spirit. And the good life, moral existence, is simply to "live in accord with nature by reason," the classic Stoic motto. The underlying theme of life is to obey the dictates of human nature and to face unflinchingly all that life (God) brings your way. Marcus Aurelius advises his readers to "wake up your mind that nothing is of any import save to do what your own nature directs, and to bear what the world's Nature sends you" (12:32). Life is a play. It is real, then? Yes, quite real, but it has a script, and you have a role: play it well.

How true it is that the same scenario seems to be played over and over again, only with different actors taking the roles! By stressing this, Marcus Aurelius tried to get his readers not to take themselves and their activities over seriously, as if you were Zeus's gift to the world, as if the fate of the world hung on your plans, as if no one had ever accomplished what you aim for. If we realize we are simply doing what all of our species do, we will see it as no less worth doing, but we will gain a wise perspective on it.

And we may learn to stop taking certain trivial things so seriously. Small talk, for example: it is unavoidable in certain circumstances and better than strained silence, but it is purely ritual in nature, nothing beyond an exchange of passwords and banalities, like a complicated but memorized fraternity handshake. Isn't it frightening to realize that you have whole relationships that are *nothing but exchanges of small talk?* Whole categories of behavior are empty rituals. An experiment might help to prove the point. Why don't you turn on your television and find an afternoon talk show? Now turn down the sound. You are not missing anything. In fact, if you taped the audio from yesterday's show and played it back now, you would see virtually *no difference.* The topic changes each day, from one lurid improbability to another, but little information is dispensed, no insight gained. The soundbite nature of the format takes care of that. No important subject could be explored in any depth between commercials and within the thirty-second limit before the next question. No, such shows are all about *audience* performance, and the performance is the same on every show. No matter what the ostensible topic, you can count on someone getting up to say "He's so right! I had that problem and here's what happened to *me....* " Someone else will get up and criticize the guest's position from the standpoint of the Bible, someone else just because it's a new idea and therefore can't be worth much. A young "meathead" (like Mike on *All in the Family*) will ask indignantly how the panel can spend so much effort on such questions when there are the much more serious problems of drugs and the environment, etc. You get the idea. You see one such show, you've seen 'em all. Is it worth continuing to watch?

Though small talk is not exactly the stuff of which vital relationships are made, it is indeed a necessary tool. As we said above, you sometimes need it as a buffer. And "Limelight" reflects momentarily on this aspect of life as a performance. Notice, by the way, that in two lines the song speaks of *living* in the limelight and *living* in a fisheye lens. If the whole point of the song were to bemoan the dangers facing literal stage performers, one might have expected to find *"Being* in the limelight," *"Captured by* the fisheye lens," or some such. "Living" onstage implies what this Shakespeare paraphrase makes explicit: all the world's indeed a stage and we are merely players. The original, from *As You Like It*, Act 2, Scene 7, line 139: "All the world's a stage, and all the men and women merely players." To add "indeed" is to second the motion: Shakespeare (the great playwright, who certainly ought to know!) was right. Here the point is, Stoicism notwithstanding, life may or may not have a script, but human behavior does partake of the character of performing *even when we are not being phonies!*

Hypocrisy is one thing, but this is another. We are cast in an improbable role which we are ill-equipped to portray. The unlikely role is that of the human condition, unlikely because of the many paradoxes and absurdities that we find built into it as we experience more and more of it. Often, things in real life are so silly that no one would take them seriously if one saw them in a work of fiction. "Oh, come on! No one's *that* stupid! Nobody's *that* cruel," etc. But they are; indeed they *are!* If you have children, have you ever looked at their bright and innocent faces and wanted to say to them, "You'd never believe the world you're going to grow up in!" An unlikely one, to say the least!

Not only is our role an odd and difficult one, but, alas, we have been pushed onstage with no acting lessons! We are not prepared with sufficient tact to navigate life smoothly. "Tact" comes from the same root as "tactile." If you have tact, you have the right "touch" with people. You know how to play the role to perfection. Again, life's a play, perhaps a tragedy or a comedy depending on our acting ability.

Lacking tact, we must put up barriers to protect ourselves, to render us less vulnerable to those who would take advantage of us or influence us badly. These barriers may be avoidance postures ("Okay, I've learned my lesson! I'm never again dating a woman who hates her father, since sooner or later she'll take it out on me!"). But our barriers are perhaps more often masks, the stylized faces we habitually present to certain individuals or in certain circumstances. Sociologist Erving Goffman devoted a fascinating book to this phenomenon, *The Presentation of Self in Everyday Life.* Here are a few remarks from his preface: "The perspective employed in this report is that of the theatrical performance; the principles derived are dramaturgical ones. I shall consider the way in which the individual in ordinary work situations presents himself and his activity to others, the ways in which he guides and controls the impression they form of him, and the kinds of things he may and may not do while sustaining his performance before them."

Isn't it true that you adopt, probably without thinking about it, a different persona (Latin for "actor's mask," by the way!) to interact with your parents, your teacher, your boss, and with different friends? You have a set of options, responses, and ways of relating to each one. With some friends, more laid-back ones, you act *and feel* like a leader or an authority. With more outgoing or dynamic ones, you slip automatically into the role of a passive follower. It can be quite startling suddenly to realize there are two (or more) such different versions of you. You are play-acting, though you are entirely sincere in each case. You are just playing a different role in each case, the role of you as cast by the particular friend to whom you have learned to relate in a particular way.

Rush says that on the one hand we are performers and portrayers, and on the other hand we are each other's audience outside the gilded cage. Even outside the obviously artificial stage of a concert hall or drama theater, we inevitably play our roles, always acting. For whom? We are each other's audience. Again, this is exactly like sociologist Goffman: "On the stage one player represents himself in the guise of a character to characters projected by other players; the audience constitutes a third party to the interaction—one that is essential and yet, if the stage performance were real, one that would not be there. In real life, the three parties are compressed into two; the part one individual plays is tailored to the parts played by the others present, and yet these others also constitute the audience."

In other words, in a play upon a literal stage, all the actors are accomplices in the scheme; it is only the audience who is being fooled, so to speak. There is a shared knowledge among the cast. One actor feels secure knowing that his dialogue partner will say the lines he expects, the lines he will know how to answer, thanks to the script. But in real life we are totally alone! Every other actor is our audience, and we are his! We are all in an improvisational troupe, and our career depends on coming up with a clever rejoinder *fast!* No wonder it's so hard to get good reviews!

But living on a lighted stage, as we all do since it is the inevitable human condition, requires us to put up barriers of another kind as well. Here Rush has brushed up against the insight of playwright and film director Ingmar Bergman, who has compared life to the theater as macrocosm to microcosm perhaps more profoundly than anyone else. Bergman's last film, *Fanny and Alexander* (1984), recounted the joys and tragedies of a theatrical family in turn-of-the-century Sweden. The Ekdahl family owns and operates the town theater, and their life together seems to be a series of comic and tragic plays. Central to the plot is the struggle of young Alexander, whose newly-widowed mother, an actress, has married a severe and fanatical bishop. At one point his mother reproves Alexander, "Don't act Hamlet, my son. I am not Queen Gertrude, your kind stepfather is no king of Denmark, and this is not Elsinore Castle, even if it does look gloomy." Of course she has exactly described the situation even as she denies it! Life imitates art imitates life, etc. The whole film is a working out of this theme. Near the beginning of the film, the Ekdahls and their actors have just rung down the curtain on the annual Christmas play. Family patriarch and theater owner Oscar Ekdahl gives the customary speech: "I love this little world inside the thick walls of this playhouse. And I'm fond of the people who work in this little world. Outside is the big world, and sometimes the little world succeeds for a moment in reflecting the big world, so that we understand it better." In fact that is exactly the relevance of the Hamlet comparison later in the movie: the analogy between the real life scenario and the Shakespeare play should have alerted Alexander's mother to the true nature of the situation.

Oscar continues: "Or is it perhaps that we give the people who come here the chance of forgetting for a while the harsh world outside.

Our theater is a small room of orderliness, routine, conscientiousness, and love." At the end of the film, Oscar's brother Gustav Adolf gives a matching speech. The awful, Hamlet-like ordeal has been resolved, and, in large measure, the family's happiness has been restored, though not without heavy costs. Relieved, Gustav Adolf says:

> "We might as well ignore the big things. We must
> live in the little, the little world. We shall be content
> with that and cultivate it and make the best of it.
> Suddenly death strikes, suddenly the abyss opens,
> suddenly the storm howls and disaster is upon us—all
> that we know. But let us not think of all that unpleas-
> antness.... Therefore it is necessary, and not in the
> least shameful, to take pleasure in *the little world*,
> good food, gentle smiles, fruit-trees in bloom,
> waltzes."

Just so: to erect barriers so as to keep oneself intact is precisely to raise up "the thick walls of the playhouse," the selective creation of a cloistered microcosm in which one can live at peace. It is futile to refuse to believe that sorrow and death will never strike you, but what good will it do to live in constant dread of them? If you are to live in the world at all, you must carve out a pleasant and livable space within it for yourself. If you enjoy life and can even make it more enjoyable, don't feel guilty for walling out the screams of misery. There are moments, seasons, when you ought to hear them and heed them. Perhaps you can help them. But you will be or do no good to anyone unless you have a sub-world of your own, a private stage on which to play out the grand drama of your destiny.

There is yet one hint more to pursue. "Limelight"'s stage images suggest that we can escape real life by hypocritical or vicarious role-playing. They suggest that even when sincere, life is largely drama and acting, that we should discern and follow its script, that we should act with tact or judiciously employ masks. But beyond these two options of theater as less real than life and theater as the technique of real life, it is possible to discern a third message: that life seems, like Plato's allegorical cave, a mere shadowplay when compared to a grander design that transcends it. "Real life" is itself less real than something standing behind and above it.

Listen again to the opening stanza of the song with this possibility in mind. The gilded cage, an image we have so far neglected, becomes relevant here. The phrase has always been used to refer to pleasant but demeaning confinement. Women have long been regarded with special esteem by men, but that very esteem had the effect of imprisoning them within men's stereotypes. The qualities, real or imagined, for which women were cherished and honored were the ones men thought made women unfit to play an equal role in the world. "Bless the ladies for their sentimentality! Where would we be without them? But let them run a company or a country? Absurd! They'd never have the hard-nosed realism necessary for the job!" The flip side of chivalry was chauvinism.

A gilded cage is a prettified cell, being under house arrest but with room service to mollify you. Is "real life" like that? Is there perhaps, beyond it, a world of infinite wonder accessible only to dreamers and mystics? As Aldous Huxley points out in *The Doors of Perception,* visionaries of all ages and nations have consistently described the exotic terrain of their visions as glowing with a deeper, more vivid, more *substantial* reality, which makes our own seem to be the dream by contrast. H. P. Lovecraft's sonnet "Alienation" seems to parallel the first stanza of "Limelight" interpreted this way:

> His solid flesh had never been away,
> For each dawn found him in his usual place,
> But every night his spirit loved to race
> Through gulfs and worlds remote from common day.
> He had seen Yaddith, yet retained his mind,
> And come back safely from the Ghooric zone,
> When one still night across curved space was thrown
> That beckoning piping from the voids behind.
>
> He waked that morning as an older man,
> And nothing since has looked the same to him.
> Objects around float nebulous and dim—
> False phantom trifles of some vaster plan.
> His folk and friends are now an alien throng
> To which he struggles vainly to belong.

Lovecraft, especially in his sonnets, espoused a kind of mysticism of *place* and of the *past* which we will see in Rush's songs "The Camera Eye" and "Tai Shan."

"The Camera Eye"

"The Camera Eye," as the title should make clear, is a direct sequel to "Limelight." Now something else is caught in the camera eye, caught by a wide-angle watcher. There is a basic thematic continuity between the previous song and this one, though it is not so obvious. The two sections of "The Camera Eye" each depict a city, the New York of today and the London of yesterday. As we will see, London is intended as the past self of New York, an earlier incarnation, as it were.

The description of Manhattan here is strongly reminiscent of that given more briefly in "Subdivisions." Drawn in stark details here is the familiar rat race. In fact, here the streets of Manhattan look almost like a laboratory maze for rats. It is clear that the grim-faced New Yorkers, deadly intent about their own business, have insufficient tact; they have put up barriers to keep themselves intact. One must pass the annoying panhandlers, the clownish whores, the curbside hawkers, the whispering crack-peddlers, with a glance neither to the right nor to the left, unless you want to end up as some kind of dubious statistic. And you might watch your back on the subway platform, too.

In "Subdivisions" it was implied that the city, for all of its apparent wildness, could become as rigidly structured as the suburbs with their geometric order. Note now that the New Yorkers move as an angular mass, pacing in rhythm—in other words, they are marching in rigid formation like a phalanx of troops! Their pace is terrific; they race against the nightfall, so as to be up early the next morning for another day of the same grind. They chase, plunging head-first, their headlong rush checked only by the "Don't Walk" light to make way momentarily for a rival legion of rushing commuters in cars. Though as individuals each one has a destination, our viewing them as a mass creates the illusion that the sprawling amorphous mob stampedes aimlessly, washing like a floodtide back and forth through the city, or like a herd of cattle driven to panic by a thunderstorm, racing this way and that in their frenzy. An illusion? Perhaps. But then perhaps the big picture tells the true story. You have to see it in the wide-angle lens to get the proper perspective on the matter. Then you see that you are a Digital Man among Digital Men. Indeed, observing them, one can hardly resist being caught up in their line of march. Listening to the song, one's feet catch the pulse and repeat the purposeful stride.

The song moves to a description of the city itself, the stage upon which the rushing commuters are the players. The tops of the buildings are lost in their limitless rise—skyscrapers which, given the leaden skies, do not appear as spires straining at their roots as if to take off like so many rockets straining to leap toward the North Star. No, since we cannot see their tops, but only a ceiling of dull grey above, we are made to feel like the toiling troglodyte slaves in the silent film *Metropolis*, lost to the sunlight many levels *below* the city. No sky, no hope. How tragic, since the city, a world in itself, is full of possibilities. Beholding it, one can scarcely avoid seeing the paradox: the sense of possibilities juxtaposed with, perhaps throttled by, the wrench of hard realities. It may seem like a double exposure, but in fact that is exactly the picture received by the camera eye. There is no distortion. The camera's focus is sharp in the city.

This contrast between possibilities and hard realities in the city forms the division point between the two sections of the song. Section I depicts the hard realities, Section II, the possibilities. Exactly the same contrast is drawn by H. P. Lovecraft in his short story "He," in a semi-autobiographical monument to his unhappy "New York Exile." Lovecraft was a native of Providence, Rhode Island, specifically of the Colonial-and-Victorian era College Hill section of East Providence. As the sonnet quoted on his memorial marker at the Brown University John Hay Library reads,

> I never can be tied to raw, new things.
> For I first saw the light in an old town,
> Where from my window huddled roofs sloped down
> To a quaint harbor rich with visionings.
> Streets with carved doorways where the sunset beams
> Flooded old fanlights and small windowpanes,
> And Georgian steeples topped with gilded vanes—
> These were the sights that shaped my childhood
>   dreams
>
>   ("Background").

Lovecraft lived for a few years in New York City, a prospect he first greeted with eagerness, but soon it palled on him. The possibility and the reality of New York proved to be two quite different things.

> The disillusion had been gradual. Coming for the first time upon the town, I had seen in the sunset from a bridge, majestic above its waters, its incredible peaks and pyramids rising flower-like and delicate from pools of violet mist to play with the flaming golden clouds and the first stars of evening. Then it had lighted up window by window above the shimmering tides where lanterns nodded and glided and deep horns bayed weird harmonies, and itself became a starry firmament of dream, redolent of faery music, and one with the marvels of Carcassone and Samarcand and El Dorado and all the glorious and half-fabulous cities.

However,

> Garish daylight showed only squalor and alienage and the noxious elephantiasis of climbing, spreading stone where the moon had hinted of loveliness and elder magic; and the throngs of people that seethed through the flume-like streets were...strangers with hardened faces and narrow eyes, shrewd strangers without dreams..., who could never mean aught to a...man...

with the love of fair green lanes and white New England village steeples in his heart.

The passage has been quoted at such length so you can see for yourself how precisely Lovecraft's and Peart's pictures of the city coincide, down to a series of the very same images: the ambivalent skyscrapers, the sense of betrayed possibility, masses of hurrying, stone-faced strangers without dreams, and the revelation of all this via the sharp focus of garish daylight. And Lovecraft's prose helps us interpret the second section of Rush's song, the part dealing with the lost and lurking possibility.

What Lovecraft beheld as he approached the city from afar, the "elder magic" of a half-fabulous castle, Peart describes in exactly parallel terms. He speaks of the city redolent of life's ancient tales (*e.g.*, of El Dorado, Samarcand, Carcassone), steeped in the history of London. Lovecraft, too, chooses yesterday's London as his point of comparison and contrast with today's New York:

> I saw at last a fearful truth which no one had ever dared to breathe before—the unwhisperable secret of secrets—the fact that this city of stone and stridor is not a sentient perpetration of old New York as London is of Old London and Paris of Old Paris, but that it is in fact quite dead.

To Lovecraft's pools of violet mist and flaming golden clouds correspond Peart's green and grey washes in a wispy white veil. Both faery panoramas are the lingering promise of the past, now left fallow. Peart's wispy white veil is the mist of a light rain which softens the hard, sharp lines of reality, allowing an inner radiance to shine forth warmly. It is the rain-mist image which most overtly joins the two sections of the song. In Section I we read that the New Yorkers seem not to notice a soft spring rain like the rain in an English countryside, lightly and endlessly filtering down from the leaden sky. This is followed in Section II by these images which would make entire sense following directly upon those just mentioned, which perhaps they are intended to do as a kind of continued refrain: can they indeed remain oblivious to this quality of light unique to city streets? Who is Peart talking about? There is no viable referent in Section II. The only people mentioned in the song are the New Yorkers of Section I. It is they who remain oblivious to this misty radiance of epic-historical depth. Though it lies spread out all around them, it is a heritage and a promise they cannot pause to appreciate.

This mist, this wispy white veil, this peculiar quality of light is exactly parallel to what Lovecraft describes in his sonnet "Continuity":

> There is in certain ancient things a trace
> Of some dim essence—more than form or weight;
> A tenuous aether, indeterminate,
> Yet linked with all the laws of time and space.
> A faint, veiled sign of continuities
> That outward eyes can never quite descry;
> Of locked dimensions harboring years gone by,
> And out of reach except for hidden keys.
> It moves me most when slanting sunbeams glow
> On old farm buildings set against a hill,
> And paint with life the shapes which linger still
> From centuries less a dream than this we know.
> In that strange light I feel I am not far
> From that fixt mass whose sides the ages are.

That mass, Eternity, is the reality beyond the gilded cage of which we heard in "Limelight." The clue, the key to it, is the past as evoked by certain places if we are not insensitive to their hints. The past remains as a depth dimension invisible to those Digital Men and Women who are attuned only to change. They are sadly oblivious to this quality. The sidewalks may teem with intense energy because of their headlong, lemming-like rush, but the city remains eerily calm in this violent sea. It has, it knows, its grander past, and this depth lends it the calm serenity of the eye of the storm. In the midst of the violent sea we can make out the pools of violet mist if our focus is sharp enough.

"Tai Shan"

The idea of a mysticism of *place* and *past* occurs again with even greater clarity in "Tai Shan" (*Hold Your Fire*, 1987), where a visit, really a pilgrimage, to China leads to an encounter with China's *genius loci* (the spirit of the place). This song is as close to overt religiosity as Rush ever gets. One reaches the crest of Tai Shan, the sacred mountain, where, as at Sinai, a revelation will be vouchsafed, by climbing seven thousand steps (reminiscent of the seven thousand onyx steps Lovecraft's character Randolph Carter must *descend* to reach the Gates of Deeper Slumber and pass into the Dream World). Once there, the pilgrim senses something will happen; a kind of psychic ozone smell presages it, a sense of magic in the air. Lovecraft felt it, too:

> There is a breathless, vague expectancy,
> As of vast ancient pomps I half-recall,
> Of wild adventures, uncorporeal,
> Ecstasy-fraught, and as a day-dream free.
> ("Expectancy")

It was in autumn's golden light that the ascent of the mountain took place in the peaceful haze of harvest time; there is the peculiar quality of light from "The Camera Eye" by whose glow deeper things are seen. And Lovecraft, too, knew the magic of that season:

> It is a certain hour of twilight glooms
> Mostly in autumn, when the star-wind pours
> Down hilltop streets, deserted out of doors,
> But showing early lamplight from snug rooms.
> The dead leaves rush in strange, fantastic twists,
> And chimney-smoke whirls round with alien grace
> Heeding geometries of outer space,
> While Fomalhaut peers in through southward mists.
>
> ("Star-Winds")

In "Tai Shan," too, clouds surround the summit, a wind blows stiff and chill in and out among the silent temples with their gold-leaf inscriptions. What wind is that but Lovecraft's star-wind? And the delicate beauty of ancient China, a kind of timeless antechamber of eternity already upon earth, formed the setting for some of Lovecraft's visions, too:

> Beyond that wall, whose ancient masonry
> Reached almost to the sky in moss-thick towers,
> There would be terraced gardens, rich with flowers,
> And flutter of bird and butterfly and bee.
> There would be walls, and bridges arching over
> Warm lotus-pools reflecting temple eaves,
> And cherry trees with delicate boughs and leaves
> Against a pink sky where herons hover.
>
> ("The Gardens of Yin")

For both Peart's pilgrim and Lovecraft's dreamer, the sight of ancient China's temples acts as the catalyst for a galvanizing revelation, because in both cases the sight strikes a reverberating gong-note deep within. Somewhere down in the instincts something primitive strikes root.

> All would be there, for had not old dreams flung
> Open the gate to that stone-lantern maze
> Where drowsy streams spin out their winding ways,
> Trailed by green vines from bending branches hung?
>
> ("The Gardens of Yin")

The revelation breaks; Peart's narrator stands transfixed like a mystic when the clouds divide, allowing a single moment of far-penetrating vision. Again Lovecraft uses the same image:

> I cannot tell why some things hold for me
> A sense of unplumbed marvels to befall,
> Or of a rift in the horizon's wall
> Opening to worlds where only gods can be.
>
>   ("Expectancy")

Of course the metaphor of the clouds parting, to form a "rift in the horizon's wall," really denotes the sudden penetration of the clouds that usually stop the *mind* from seeing *truth*. What, then, is the truth now seen with clarity? China chants an eternal song which imparts to the visionary a glimpse of a presence spanning forty centuries. For Lovecraft, it is the familiar landscape of his beloved Providence, but the effect is the same. The sight of the ancient place

> Cannot but loose the hold of flimsier wraiths
> That flit with shifting ways and muddled faiths
> Across the changeless wails of earth and heaven.
> They cut the moment's thongs and leave me free
> To stand alone before eternity.

Peart's visionary sees a presence spanning forty centuries. The wording implies that what he sees not only subsists through the duration of four thousand years, but stands changelessly above them. He sees in a timeless moment Eternity itself, clothed in China's silks. He sees what Lovecraft describes as "the fixt mass whose sides the ages are" ("Continuity").

Trapped in a ceaseless flow of change we may be, members of a herd that stampedes to and fro. There is just no opting out of it. But we may become like "Tom Sawyer," like the mystic atop the mountain. We may be able to freeze this moment a little bit longer in our perception, so that certain places and remembered times become for us momentary catalysts for a glimpse beyond the rushing clouds of change. We may not be able finally to escape the gilded cage which spins around us like a merry-go-round, its bars seeming to merge together into a solid wall. But if we try, we can gain a split-second peek through those bars and come to be in touch with some reality beyond it.

IV.

CASTLES IN THE DISTANCE

Some Rock groups are known for a particular theme or emphasis that shows up through most of their work. This is probably the minority, since most groups seem dedicated to cranking out puerile love-songs, magnifying puppy-love to cosmic proportions with their amplification and sound effects. Protest music is rarer nowadays than in the Sixties, but you do hear some now and again. As the present book ought to make clear, Rush cannot be neatly pigeonholed, and it would be wrong to call them a protest group. Nonetheless, a political dimension is not absent from their work. In this chapter, we will examine a few songs dealing with the process of social change and about Rush's views on nationalism and internationalism. Before we get started, let's just remind ourselves that all the songs about social conformity and the dangers of institutions are no less political, and those songs should be kept in mind here, too.

"A Farewell to Kings"

We begin with "A Farewell to Kings," the title song of Rush's 1977 album. This song warns of social/governmental decline, a sad falling away from a noble heritage. Will future historians confirm the singer's suspicions that this present period is one of fatal decay? If so, how will it have happened? People have lost touch both with their national destiny and with their own nobler instincts. As to the former, it is not that our leaders have seized the wheel and purposely steered us in the wrong direction, but rather that they simply abdicated their responsibility to keep things on a straight course, to correct any drift. They are like the tipsy captain of an oil tanker who drinks himself silly and just lets the ship run aground where it will. The troubles that threaten our civilization (hate-filled cities, hearts withered from believing too many lies) have sprung from seeds that we let grow. No one is accused of intentionally *planting* such seeds, not even the leaders. Rather, perhaps as in the Parable of the Wheat and the Tares, when peculiar-looking stuff starts coming up in the field, everyone is at first puzzled ("Sir, did you not sow good seed in your field?"), until the realization dawns,

"An enemy has done this" (Matthew 13:27-28). But the leaders' job was to root them up, keep them under control, deal with the evil fruit. They haven't. They were too busy fiddling while Rome burned, too busy voting themselves raises and running for cover whenever a vote on a controversial issue would have required them to make an unpopular decision. Government by cowardice, venality, and laziness has cast our society adrift. The path to historic greatness once trod vigorously by the democracies of the West now lies covered with weeds. It was an inexorable downturn when we turned our gaze from the castles in the distance and instead cast down our eyes along the path of least resistance. "For wide is the gate, and broad is the way that leads to destruction, and many there are who go in" (Matthew 7:13).

What sort of leaders are these? They are living caricatures, parodies, distortions. Scheming demons who dress in kingly guise and beat down the multitudes are *not* proper kings, but only *disguised* as such. Their advisors? The days are gone when a country might be ruled by a Charlemagne advised by an Alcuin of York, a King Hezekiah counseled by a Prophet Isaiah, an Arthur advised by a Merlin. No, the demon-kings scoff at the wise and give their place to hypocrites who slander the hallowed halls of Truth, *i.e.*, philosophical schools, courtrooms, churches, and temples. These men slander the ivied halls of Truth by giving them a bad reputation with their wretched behavior. "Hypocrite" is a Greek word for "play-actor," a phony. Like today's heads of state, their advisors are fakes, having ousted the genuine articles. The song evokes the biblical image of the Antichrist and his false prophet: "And I beheld another beast coming up out of the earth; and he had two horns like a lamb, and he spoke like a dragon. And he exercises all the power of the first beast before him, and causes the earth and those who dwell on it to worship the first beast" (Revelations 13:11-12).

How did we start with Locke, Rousseau, Jefferson, and Madison—and end up like this? We, too, it seems, have been following the path of least resistance. We let the kings get away with murder, perhaps because of our own cynicism or our self-absorption. Or perhaps because we have let our own sensibilities atrophy. Whose are the withered hearts, but ours? We have forgotten how to feel what's right and wrong and must now try, in the eleventh hour, to relearn it before it's too late.

Perhaps we lost touch with our moral instincts by means of the belief that politics involves compromise in an imperfect world. It surely does; we mustn't be naïve. Sometimes you do have to ally yourself with a Stalin to fight a Hitler. But we start sliding down the slippery slope. We go from thinking you have to bend the rules to thinking there are no rules, from situational ethics to no ethics at all. One need not make such a step. Logic doesn't force you to. But we're talking about the path of least resistance, remember? It sure is easy to let everything slide. In fact, the more you start to slip the easier it *becomes* to slip, because your standards change. What you were once ashamed of now looks pretty good to you, since in the meantime you've sunk to an even *lower* level, and from there it doesn't look so bad. With your standards thus lowered, your conscience thinks it has less to bother you about, so it takes a little nap. And there you are, merrily cruising down that broad and winding path to destruction.

If it was our languid moral torpor which allowed our leadership to decline so disastrously, we will have to begin to reverse the process by regaining our moral sensitivity. We ourselves may not be designed to govern or to lead, so our task is to find the minds that made us strong—more like Jefferson and Madison, if they are available! And what will we need them to do? Provide *moral*, not just pragmatic leadership. The sacrifice of the former to the latter is what caused the problem in the first place! The poison in power, remember, kills any higher principles ("Grand Designs"). We need to, we must, find the minds needed to lead us closer to the heart, to moral sensitivity in national life. If we can, if they are out there, the history books may turn out differently. We may make it to those castles in the distance after all.

As you might well guess, "Closer to the Heart" is the direct continuation of "A Farewell to Kings" (it is surely a continuation of *something*, since it begins with the word "And"!). However, we immediately seem to find an inconsistency. In view of the kiss-off to demon-kings in the first song, it is a surprise to discover in the second that it is precisely the men who hold high places who must take the lead in moulding a new reality closer to the heart. This sounds like a glaring contradiction, but really it all fits fine. These men in high places are not the discredited demon-kings (a hearty "good-riddance" to them!), but rather the minds that will make us strong again, who will lead us closer to the heart. They will not beat down but lift up the multitude.

> The kings of the Gentiles exercise lordship over them;
> and those who exercise authority over them are called
> benefactors. But it shall not be so among you; but he
> who is greatest among you, let him be as the younger;
> and he who is chief, as he who serves. (Luke 22:25-
> 26)

These new leaders must set the tone for everyone else, but all must do their parts. All must let the new spirit permeate their efforts. Both blacksmith and sculptor alike reflect it in their art. Each in his own way forges his creativity closer to the heart. And, thank God, the hypocrites have been turned out of the Halls of Truth, no longer to soil them by their presence. The wise are back in their proper positions. The philosopher, like the ploughman, must accept his responsibility to help sow a new mentality closer to the heart. The two roles are really the same: the philosopher is the ploughman. "The sower sows the word" (Mark 4:14), literally the Logos. The Stoics, too, spoke of *logou spermatikoi*, "seeds of reason," the organizing principle in all things. Here the philosopher sows them to reap the crop of a new mentality.

"Distant Early Warning"

In subsequent songs, we seem to sense less hope for sweeping political renewal, more of a sense of chastened naïveté, and a realization that compromise with the entrenched powers is the best one can hope for, at least until those powers die off and can be replaced by a "New World Man." In "Distant Early Warning" (*Grace Under Pressure*, 1984). There is a definite feeling of bemusement and frustration. The lyrics convey world-weariness, helplessness. There are problems aplenty, that's for sure; one feels the chill of the proverbial "ill wind that blows no good." It blows across the cities of the plain—the generic name for Sodom and Gomorrah and their suburbs (in Genesis, Chapter 19), destroyed by Jehovah in a rain of fire and sulphur for their wickedness. Are we due the same fate? Will our environmental heedlessness doom us? A sign posted at the reservoir warns: no swimming in the heavy water—unless you want to emerge an atomic mutant. And there'll be no singing in the acid rain—even Gene Kelly would have trouble doing his famous song and dance with that bulky environmental suit he'd have to wear!

What is to be done? Gone are the New Left certainties of the Sixties. It no longer seems so simple. The minds that made us strong had to learn that the hard way, as when Thomas Jefferson had to agree to erase the emancipation of slaves from the Declaration of Independence before Virginia would sign it.

We used to see the issues in the stark blacks and whites of youth, before we realized just how ambiguous the world is, how difficult it is to tell the demon-kings and hypocrites on the one hand from the great minds and wise men on the other. It is a rite of passage, essentially no different from a high-school graduation exercise or a sweet sixteen party or a bar mitzvah, to embrace Communism, or to join the Young Republicans, the lefts and rights/rites of passage. The rhetoric of both makes the issues black and white, with no confusing shades of grey. Only an adolescent can believe *that!*

One eventually outgrows such immature zeal, but not without a shock. Who can face the knowledge that what he took to be the truth is not the truth after all? That the party-line to which you once pledged allegiance is not what it's cracked up to be? That it is obsolete, not absolute, as you thought in your youthful enthusiasm. The day comes when hard experience (perhaps the bullets of Kent State) disabuses us of our wide-eyed zeal. We mourn for those days of youthful conviction and undimmed optimism, much as King David wept for his son Absalom, the heir to his throne, who could not wait his turn and tried to seize power, finally getting killed in the attempt. David cried, "O my son Absalom, my son, my son Absalom! Would to God I had died for thee, O Absalom, my son, my son!" (II Samuel 18:33). We, too, have lost a young revolutionary: the idealistic person we were in our youth. Hence the final words of the song. Alas, the innocence slips away ("Time Stand Still").

"Second Nature"

"Second Nature" (*Hold Your Fire*, 1987) sounds like a more sober, older-and-wiser version of "Farewell to Kings," after the painful maturation of "Distant Early Warning." Now the thought is not to replace the demon-kings with a flock of new Jeffersons and Lockes, but rather to negotiate with the Powers that be. The song presents itself not as a rallying cry for rebellion, not as a list of demands, but rather as an invitation to the bargaining table. In "Closer to the Heart" we heard that those in high places must take the lead in shaping a new reality closer to the heart, but, alas, they are not doing any such thing! Hence this memorandum to a higher office, this open letter to a god, a king, a head of state, a captain of industry.

The complaint against the authorities, like that in "Distant Early Warning," is more specific than in "A Farewell to Kings" and "Closer to the Heart." These two songs are concerned pointedly with the environment. The point here is that nature is under attack by industry, and it is amazing that even the greedy exploiters cannot see the fatal foolishness in this! Where do you plan to spend all that money you've made helping to turn Mother Earth into a blackened, dessicated corpse? Environmental concern ought to be second nature; in other words, it shouldn't really require any long process of reflection to see the error in committing matricide against Mother Nature!

Progress is not long on patience. We can't afford to stop and protect the environment, developers say! We have to get those minerals out of the hills now, so let's crank up those plutonium plants, and we'll figure out what to do with the heavy water (beyond putting up a NO SWIMMING sign) later. The drawing aside of the Iron Curtain has demonstrated the cost of hell-bent industrial modernization. East Germany, the most advanced of the East European countries, turned out to be a post-apocalyptic dead zone, with "silver lakes" scummed with a metallic film of toxic wastes, with air quality many times over the danger limit. Third World countries like Brazil and the Malagasy Republic chop down their ancient rain forests because they need to clear the land *now*, environment be damned! To be sure, progress has no patience, but sooner or later, *something's* got to give: if not the pace of progress, then the viability of the environment.

"Second Nature" echoes with the anguish of impotent protest. The captains of industry are too many captains steering us wrong. So much for the hope of your being the captain, me charting the course! It's a crueler world than we thought. The rule of Big Money is hard to buck. The best we can hope for is half a loaf, but it's better than none. Compromise is not to be despised if it's all you can get.

Yet this new realism brings with it a new candor about one's own role, one's own responsibility for the mess. Who is not a polluter, an accomplice in a polluting commercial society? Is your so-righteous indignation ever directed at yourself? So it's easier to take your baby to that Greenpeace rally, you wrap her up in a plastic diaper that will never decompose in a whole geological age? Do you hand out leaflets to protest pollution, heedless of their destination as street litter? The rally for the twentieth anniversary of Earth Day left behind *tons* of trash!

Damn hard to lay the blame.

"Territories"

In "Territories" (*Grace Under Pressure*, 1985), the political focus shifts from national to international, from problems here at home to the issue of our attitude toward the rest of the world. "Territories" bemoans nationalism that has become chauvinism, jingoism. The clear implication is that nationalism cannot help leading to chauvinism, or even that there is no difference between the two.

The song opens with a mention of the Middle Kingdom between Heaven and Earth. The Middle Kingdom, or Central Kingdom, is the literal translation of the Chinese name for China, Chung-Kuo. The name denotes ethnocentrism, thinking your own nation is central in importance, all others being merely peripheral. The Chinese historically viewed other nations as barbarians.

In fact the barbarians themselves may have viewed it the same way! Whenever a "barbarian" horde swept into and overran China, establishing their own dynasty, they did not bring the sublime Chinese culture down in ruins, but rather embraced it and ruled as *Chinese*, not as Mongols or Manchus.

We see the same phenomenon in the case of ancient Rome, who regarded subject and foreign peoples as mere barbarians ("pagan" just meant "not a Roman citizen"; "heathen" just meant "country hick from the frontier"). And when the Germanic hordes invaded and took over, what did they do? Far from dismantling the Empire and stomping it into rubble, they ruled as Caesars themselves!

The "Middle Kingdom" is seen suspended between Heaven and Earth. The allusion is probably to the similar name "Middle Earth,"

Tolkien's translation of the Norse *Midgard*, denoting earth as the mid-level between Heaven (*Asgard*) and the netherworld (*Helheim*). Peart juxtaposes the Chinese "Middle Kingdom" and the Norse "Middle Earth" to reinforce the incredible arrogance of ethnocentrism. We feel and act as if we were the only nation on earth, that we are the earth. And, of course, it's not just ancient China that the song picks on, but *everybody*, since every nation is selfishly ethnocentric to some extent. There are some people who believe wholeheartedly that the world revolves about The Gambia or Belize. We all tend to figure that our homelands are superior to those of other peoples. And this is why Peart places the "Middle Kingdom," not between Heaven and Hell, as one might expect from the Midgard association, but between Heaven and *Earth*, *i.e.*, exalted (in our eyes) above every place else on earth, above other people than the ones we know and love.

This makes it much easier to have a war, by the way; you don't realize *how many* people are being killed, since you only count the number of *your* casualties, not the enemy's. Theirs, by contrast, are so much cordwood.

They play the same territorial game in every place that has a name on a map. Choosing a name implies a certain level of self-conscious pride. And the names, like China's, are very revealing. Many American Indian tribal names, for instance, mean simply "the People" in the particular tribal language, as if no one else counted.

The various peoples and tribes are hiding behind the lines, *i.e.*, behind their borders, lines on a map, sending up warning signals. The classic example of this xenophobia would have to be Japan, which for centuries forbade any contact with outsiders, Western barbarians, until Commodore Perry simply forced his way in, unlocking Japan to foreign trade, war, and influences. Perhaps the Japanese were right the first time, since their own beautiful indigenous culture seems in danger of dissipating before Western influences. They have become a caricature of the worst parts of American Capitalist consumerism and materialism. (Of course, they have also learned to beat us at the *best* of what we do!)

One might think that the human spirit could find plenty to occupy itself in the whole wide world, the endless universe. But in fact we keep looking through the wrong end of the telescope. Instead of sweeping the cosmic ocean with the perspective of a god, which we can *do!*, we prefer a worm's eye view of matters. Such is the fixation of our nationalistic species. We scramble like ants defending their hill, oblivious to the grandeur of the starry heavens above.

We are self-isolated, at least in terms of our worldview, which gives us the central role. Self-confined in a circle drawn in the sand, we defy anyone to come and deliver us from the prison of our own making! The world could be ours, but we scurry to barricade ourselves into a tiny space. In different circles we keep holding our ground. We never touch or interact with the other. What a waste! What meaningless activity! We keep spinning round and round, going exactly nowhere, spiraling in indifferent circles. Despite the existence of entities like the United Nations, League of Nations, or World Council of Churches, we can't really get a gut feeling for what the word "international" means, so deeply lie our nationalistic-chauvinistic instincts.

No, for us to link up with another country, another territory, is to conquer it by force. The "great" era of Western colonization of Asia and the Southern Hemisphere is over now, but imperialism continues via the multinational corporations who farm out work to slave-wage workers in undeveloped countries. And countries still invade other countries; turn on the news any night: Iraq and Kuwait, Serbia and Bosnia, the feuding fragments of the Soviet Empire.

The irony is that in the very moment of even *this* kind of transcendence of national borders we are *still* mired in ethnocentrism! We despise the pagans and savages we are annexing! The invading troops dream at the evening campfires of the lands they've left behind. Back home they had better company, better food, better beer. Well, if home was so much like the Garden of Eden, what are you doing on the other side of the world? If the other territory is so "inferior" to yours, why conquer it in the first place? If it's so undesirable, why do you desire it?

But invading armies are only the beginning. They bring in their wake occupying forces, colonial administrators, and missionaries, all of whom have been notoriously arrogant, contemptuous, and insensitive to the subjugated peoples. Drunken soldiers violate the native women; intolerant missionaries stamp out indigenous creeds. Multinational companies loot natural resources.

Imperialists shoot without shame; their cause must be glorious, no? In fact, they take aim merely in the name of a piece of dirt (either the one they're defending or the one they covet). Perhaps it is merely because of trivial national differences, *e.g.*, a change of accent:

> And the Gileadites took the passages of Jordan before the Ephraimites: and when those Ephraimites who escaped said, "Let me go over"; the men of Gilead said to them, "Are you an Ephraimite?" If he said, "no," then they said to him, "Say now 'Shibboleth'": and he said "Sibboleth!": for he could not pronounce it right. Then they took hold of him, and slew him at the passages of Jordan: and at that time there fell of the Ephraimites forty and two thousand. (Judges 12:5-6)

Or you might get killed because of the color of your shirt. This seems to be a reference to the killing of anonymous soldiers unknown to you as enemies except through the arbitrary color of their uniforms. A human being behind that uniform? Yes, though it doesn't occur to us—we think we're merely blasting a blip on a video game's screen. But that blip's loved ones will grieve his loss. The classic film treatment of war's human ironies is *The Man I Killed* (also released as *Broken Lullaby*), in which a sensitive French musician, drafted into World War I, kills a German soldier, discovers his diary, and sees to his horror that the German was an artistic soul who might have been his twin.

The day of national loyalties is passing. A nobler pride is that of the one who considers himself or herself a citizen of the world. Let us be done with the Pavlovian instinct to fight like mad dogs when our flags are hoisted. These sentiments are clear enough. But why does Rush denigrate what to many of us are sacred symbols of patriotism? Is the flag of Canada, Britain, the United States merely a stained rag? Are the proud uniforms of our brave troops just different colored shirts? Is one's beloved homeland no more than a piece of dirt? No, not until we start spilling blood over them. Homeland, flag, or valor are noble things, but why is someone else's version *less* nobel? To love Britain more, must you love France less? Does love for America imply hate for China? Why on earth should it? Why not savor the heritages of *all* cultures? Why not salute *all* flags, venerate the courage of *all* soldiers? Is not the very multitude of countries, flags, armies the problem? If we loved and admired each other, why would we need borders? Why would we stingily guard resources, jealously horde wealth? Isn't it because we distrust *foreigners*? And why? Just *because* they are foreigners. And why are they foreigners? Why are there borders, which is to ask the same question? Because we *distrust* them! Xenophobia is built right into the idea of nationalism. There would be no nationalism, no separate states without it! To love most and love best the treasures symbolized by flag, uniform and country, we should dispense with the divisions marked by flag, uniform, and country!

"New World Man"

"New World Man" (*Signals*, 1982) shows how far Rock, at least Rush's, has come from the "turn on—tune in—drop out" philosophy of the Sixties. Of the three commandments of Timothy Leary just quoted, "New World Man" retains only "tune in": the New World Man is a radio receiver, all right, but he's tuning in to quite a different station.

In this song Neil Peart is talking about two things at once. He is, on the surface, focusing on a typical young, up-and-coming Canadian or American who is eager to take his place among the duties and opportunities afforded him by the affluent and advanced society he is lucky enough to have been born into. But describing this quintessential New World Man enables him to characterize that "New World" society as well. In fact, it would be safe to say that the man stands for, or personifies, the American-Canadian society. So which is the song really about? Both. America and Canada, the "New World" as opposed to Old Europe, are the sum of individuals like the one described here.

This, incidentally, implies something interesting about Rush's (or Peart's) individualism. In other songs we see more of a radical opposition between the individual with his talents on the one hand, and the collectivity which would subdue and homogenize him on the other. In songs such as "Red Alert," "Big Money," and "The Weapon," Peart argues that the gifted individuals (with whom Rush fans surely identify themselves) must strive to advance and find fulfillment against the gravity, against the current, of society. It would not go too far to say that in such songs Peart sees self-formation, self-actualization, as a process which necessarily takes the form of a combat between the individual and society which would hold him down to the level of the easily-manipulable herd. Just as the young Indian brave had to prove his manhood by killing a bear or a tribal enemy, so must today's Tom Sawyer become truly himself by winning out against Big Money's use of the Weapon to make him one more shuffling denizen of the high school halls and shopping malls.

Why the difference in approach suddenly in "New World Man"? The earlier songs clearly show the influence of Ayn Rand, whose novels and essays preached essentially the same message: only the individual can be creative; absorption in the mass means not a pooling of talent but a dilution of it. This is what one must do if one is to sink, as the "collectivists" would have us do, to the "democratic" norm, the lowest common denominator. Of course Rand is not the only thinker to espouse such views. You can find variations on this theme in the writings of Frederich Nietzsche (*The Antichrist*, *Thus Spake Zarathustra*, etc.), Colin Wilson (*The Outsider*, *Religion and the Rebel*, *The Strength to Dream*), and C. S. Lewis ("Screwtape Proposes a Toast").

This approach, this exaltation of the individual, is perhaps the fundamental assumption of political conservatism. It explains the conservative distaste for Big Government; there should ideally be only enough government to ensure the protection of each individual's pursuit of life, liberty, and happiness from possible infringements by other individuals.

"New World Man," too, seems politically conservative. But it can affirm the involvement of creative individuals in society; it envisions not liberalism's view of individuals as products of a society, its education and planning (the extreme caricature of such a society-central model would be the discredited goal of the old USSR to produce a new revolutionary "Soviet Man"), but rather the conservative, individualist ideal of a society composed of many individuals and taking its shape, flavor, and character *from them*. "Big Money," "Subdivisions," and the other songs sought to free the individual from the cloying, numb-ing, dulling grip of a conformist, mediocrity-society. "New World Man" speaks of the need to start over, building a better society from the ground up, using self-assured individualists as the building blocks. And it is they themselves who voluntarily take their places in such a so-ciety. Big Money does not easily manipulate them. This is clear from the fact that the first epithet of the New World Man is a "rebel" against the old way of doing things. The Big-Money-Red-Alert-Weapon-Witch-Hunt-way of doing things. Yet what does he want to do? He wants his chance, his turn to run the big machine—society. In fact, the young generation (especially typified by Rush fans in sympathy with the Peart philosophy) is so eager to take the reins of society that they're runners chafing at the bit. The New World Man is a signal turning green, a Go light flashing. New World Men and Women are at the starting gate, ready to take control.

It is probably no accident that the album as a whole is called *Signals*. These songs are all, so to speak, flags waving to tell the lis-tener that it's time to go. Unlike many rock bands with their irrespon-sible hedonistic creed, Rush seeks to educate and motivate its audience toward positive involvement, yet without being preachy. Rush ap-proaches the listener as a big brother might—someone still close enough to you in age that you can't write him off as someone from the other side of the Generation Gap. Someone who you know has been through what you're learning the hard way now, and he can make it easier for you.

The New World Man admittedly has a problem with his poi-sons. But, rest assured, he'll find a cure before it's too late. In fact, he's already cleaning up his systems, trying to keep his nature pure. First off, let's note here that we have a perfect example of the interplay between the individual and the society which takes its shape from such individuals. What are the poisons? On the individual level, the poisons are *drugs*. Peart knows good and well that the rock subculture has a large overlap with the drug subculture. In fact, in the Sixties and Sev-enties, rock songs were to a great degree simply anthems and hymns of the drug culture. Both were seen as part of the same social revolution. One suspects that much Sixties music (*e.g.*, "Acid Rock") was "in stereo" in the sense that the music was one channel and the drugs were the other: without drugs, you were receiving only one track.

But it's become clear that drugs and music were an unequal yoking. Rush is trying to break the yoke. Here is Rush, or Peart, your big brother talking. In one early Rush album, we hear a typical drug-paean of the Seventies (*e.g.*, "Passage to Bangkok," *2112*, 1976). In retrospect, this song makes you wince with embarrassment. Rush was there in the drug culture, because it seemed like part of the "young ro-manticism" still championed in this song, though later the group wised up enough to realize that the real romanticism, the approach to life which sees it as a colorful adventure, is better, more of an epic, without drugs. Drugs, after all, sooner or later leave one no more mentally alert than the beer-swilling Archie Bunker-clones of Middle America. Beer in front of the boob tube, pot in front of the stereo—what's the difference?

He has to make his own mistakes, drugs being one of them, a big one. He must learn to fix the mess he makes, and Rush is trying to help in the cleanup. His cleaning up his systems refers to the flushing out of drugs from the system of forward-looking people, though we would be too narrow in our focus if we missed a possible reference to the great upsurge in nutrition and exercise in recent years. All this, Rush says, represents a getting ready to stop "dropping out," to take in hand the challenge of the world in the next decades. One suspects that the song reflects the optimism of conservatives like Ronald Reagan and Canadian Prime Minister Brian Mulroney in the early Eighties when it seemed newly possible to stem and reverse the decline of the West that loomed darkly after Vietnam in the Seventies.

Some of the lyrics point us beyond the focus on the individual. The talk of *systems* and *nature* remind us inescapably of ecology. Society as a whole is having quite a problem with its poisons. The great industrial and scientific technology of which Rush seems both so proud and so afraid (see Chapter VII, "Machine and Man") produces terrible pollution, but Rush does not retreat into a nostalgic anti-scientific primitivism like that of Jeremy Rifkin. To do so would certainly be a type of romanticism, but we see in Rush's music what we might call a hard-headed or tough-minded romanticism. Rush sees technology as the rocketship on which the New World Man may launch himself into his exciting future. The poisons? To protect the future, we will have to clean them up. And Rush's optimistic confidence in science shows through again right here: of course we'll do it! All rumors of the decline of the West, or of its will, are premature.

We've seen that this song envisions the legions of eager, gifted New Worlders ready to pilot their society into the surging ocean of the twenty-first century and its challenges, including political ones, namely those posed by the Old World Man and the Third World Man. Who are these? The New World Man, the Canadian and American, seems fated by history to take over the world-ascendancy enjoyed by the European powers, who once dominated world-spanning commercial and political empires. But those empires were brought humbly to their knees by the two World Wars, from which the United States emerged as the great unrivaled superpower. We must learn to match the beat of the Old World Man, *i.e.*, learn to assume that position of dominance in world affairs once occupied by Spain, England, France, and Germany. We are learning: Rush is optimistic. But we still have much to learn. Like the individual young American or Canadian, our *nations* are youngsters, green, wet-behind-the-ears whippersnappers, compared to the Old World nations who, after all, have universities twice as old as our *countries,* churches and cathedrals *four* and *five* times as old! It is our youthful inexperience that poses the dangers, yet it is our youthful freshness of approach and exuberance that may allow us to succeed where the European powers failed. Both World Wars were the result of European politics going bad.

The end of Old World dominance included the breakup of their colonial empires in Asia and Africa. It is the burgeoning nations born from the colonial empires that form the Third World. Whereas "Third World" really denotes non-alignment with either the Capitalist or Communist "worlds," Peart here makes it refer to *birth* order. First is the culture of the Old World (Europe); second is America/Canada; third are the newly independent nations of the Southern Hemisphere. If we are young and impulsive compared to the Old World, we suddenly find an even newer competitor breathing down our necks, threatening to overtake us. If we are impulsive, the Third World Man is explosive. Demands for a "New Economic Order," terrorism, Khaddafy and Khomeini, are all part of the heat of the Third World Man which we had better learn how to catch if we are to hold onto the future to which our abilities entitle us. We are the future, but there is a future even more lately hatched than us!

Our military strength, our role as the world policeman, comes in view at this point. Who's got a problem with his power? Here there is no individual reference at all. He is the New World itself, Canada, America, NATO. Do we use our military strength rightly? To preserve and protect democracy in the world? Or do we still practice Teddy Roosevelt's "big stick diplomacy?" Patrolling fully-armed, the New World Man must walk a fine line and keep his self control. A case in point would be the December 1989 invasion of Panama to unseat dictator Manuel Noriega. We judged it best to eliminate a man who was not only a bloodthirsty oppressor of his own people but also a major force in smuggling drugs into America. To stop him was to try to find a cure for those poisons that give our people a problem and threaten to steal our future by robbing from a whole generation their ability to cope with a competitive and threatening world. But we walked a fine line, a tightrope. The Third World cried foul. All Latin American countries except for Panama itself said U.S. intervention was nothing but the old Yankee imperialism. Maybe it was.

We use, or refrain from using, our arsenal, because we are carefully trying to save the day for the Old World Man. How so? This is the reason for NATO. In the old days when the USSR seemed to pose a threat to European security (still the case when this song was written), we had Canadian and American troops garrisoned in Europe nose-to-nose with Warsaw Pact troops in case they should try to march across Europe and conquer our allies, Germany, France, and England, the Old World Man. When America aided Britain in her war against

Third World Argentina over the disputed Falkland Islands in 1982, the very year this album appeared, it was a case of trying to save the day for the Old World Man.

But we are also trying to pave the way for the up-and-coming Third World Man when we do things like invading the island country of Grenada to rid them of Communist usurpers who had nipped Grenadan independence in the bud, or when we prevent Saddam Hussein from wresting control of the oil-lifeline of the emerging economies of new countries. Do we have the right to do such things? It's a tightrope, but Rush is saying we have to face the challenge. Ignoring it won't make it go away. Hence the advice, the exhortation of this song. As the younger generation poises itself on the threshold of the very volatile and uncertain future, so full of potential for peril, we must be ready. Like all previous generations coming of age, we are wise enough to win the world, but easily fool enough to lose it.

V.

THE SOUNDS OF SALESMEN

In this chapter we want to consider the question of art and integrity in Rush's music. Specifically, what does Rush say about personal integrity and artistic integrity? We will find that the two are intimately related. If one is an artist of any kind, perhaps a musician like the members of Rush, one's personal and artistic integrity are the same. We will find that according to Neil Peart's lyrics, the same forces threaten both kinds of integrity, and that artistic integrity may be used as a symbol for personal integrity, and vice versa. To see this it will prove useful to compare two songs, "Something for Nothing" (1976) and "The Big Money" (1985). Though fully nine years separate the two songs, either when juxtaposed with the other serves as a revolving mirror image of the other. The contrast between them makes the point of each all the sharper.

"Something for Nothing"

"Something for Nothing" (*2112*, 1976) is one of Rush's many motivational songs, encouraging listeners to do more with their lives than listen to record albums! It is plain that one of Rush's principal artistic aims is to plant the seeds of hopes and ambitions in the minds of their fans, and equally to prod them to get up and do what is needful to realize those dreams.

"Something for Nothing" is a systematic demolition of every evasion of self-motivated action. It pictures the listener waiting for the winds of change to sweep away the clouds. Are there lowering thunderheads, impending problems you feel you cannot cope with? Do you feel that until circumstances simply change by themselves, you will have to let those gloomy prospects paralyze you? You can always tell the inveterate excuse-maker, the one who has made a vocation out of being a victim and a sadsack. When challenged, he will trot out a resume of excuses as long as your arm. He will recite them like a well-practiced liturgy, and finally he will conclude with flawless logic that his perennial defect, his characteristic inertia, was deducible from this set of roadblocks and setbacks. But he ignores one factor in his self-serving yet self-stultifying equation: his own efforts might have moved the clouds away (or might have taken him off to some cloudless region elsewhere). But effort is what he can't or won't scrape up. By now he is quite satisfied with (certainly quite *accustomed* to) waiting for circumstances to change themselves.

Are you sitting on your butt, waiting for the pot of gold to come sliding down the rainbow to your feet? You'll be waiting forever. Don't you remember the rules? To get the pot of gold, you have to *get up* and pursue the rainbow, try to climb it to its end—and then seize the gold for yourself! In countless ways of evasion and excuse-making you pass the days. A pity you can't seem to put some of that mental energy to work in making plans for your success, and stop wasting it on excuses as to why you remain a failure, a non-starter.

You don't get something for nothing. That's a cliché; everyone knows it, but you only really learn the truth of it once you stop trying to get something for nothing. You never get freedom for free—an interesting paradox! Everyone is like the indentured servants of the past, people who are not yet free but who can purchase their freedom by hard work, discharging a debt, paying off with hard labor. Do you feel trapped or enslaved by addictive habits, by oppressive circumstances, by bad breaks, anything that holds you back from the future you feel is rightly yours? Freedom for the future is possible, but no one is going to hand it to you. You must strive to win it. In fact it is probably correct to go a step further: even if someone *did* magically free you, without your own efforts, you would still be a slave inside! Real liberation, the liberty of the soul, comes only when it is you who strike off your chains! Otherwise your unreconstructed slave-mentality will just wait to find new excuses to evade the challenges of freedom.

How much more true is this in the case of *wisdom*: no one gets wise with the sleep still in his eyes. Even if you have grand dreams, you have to wake up and *act* in order to realize them! It is possible to soak up some knowledge, some facts, by passive reception, though perhaps not much worth knowing. But a passive acquisition of *wisdom* is out of the question. Wisdom can only come through *experience*, the trial-and-effort process of aggressive engagement with life. Is this theory sound? Is that advice true to life? Were your parents or your rabbi correct? Are the ideas Rush sings about good ones? You will never know until you try them out.

> I went by the field of the slothful
> and by the vineyard of the man void of understanding;
> and, lo, it was all grown over with thorns
> and nettles had covered the face thereof,
> and the stone wall thereof was broken down.
> Then I saw, and considered it well;
> I looked upon it, and received instruction.
> "Yet a little sleep, a little slumber,

a little folding of the
hands to sleep;"
So shall your poverty come like one who hastens, and
your want like an armed man.

(Proverbs 24:30-34)

Here is the same linkage: laziness and lack of *wisdom.*

Again, are you waiting for someone to knock at the door with a handy plan to turn your world around? No one is likely to come and do that for you; the only ones you can expect to call on you are Poverty and Want, as in the Proverb. Are you looking for an open door? You will find none opening on where you want to be; you'll only make progress by *opening some doors yourself.* If all the career options your parents or guidance counselors set before you seem dull, if you would have to sell out in order to follow those options, then these open doors lead nowhere for you. You will have to strike out on your own and find something *else,* open a new door. See what use you can make of your talents, with or without the door-opening assistance of others.

Are you seeking an answer to the questions you've found? Be careful where you look! Your answer is already inside your head. Let it guide you along. As Socrates demonstrated to Meno many centuries ago, the truth is already implicit within and needs only to be teased out by a series of leading questions that will cause the mind to sharpen *itself* so it may realize its own answers. This is not to say one ought to spurn the knowledge offered by others; there is no one you cannot learn from. But it *does* mean you are no blank slate, that your mind is not an empty square to be filled up by the first person to get to it with a piece of chalk. It is not good enough to be satisfied with whatever your parents and teachers told you, though they were right to tell you the best they knew. It is your job to evaluate what you've been told and what else you can learn. It is your duty to put all ideas to the test in the laboratory of experience. No one can do these things for you, and until you do, you will have no right to claim you've found any answers.

The point of the whole song, though expressed in different ways, is that you must be inner-directed, and not outer-directed, if you are ever to follow your dreams to their fruition. Again, that doesn't mean automatic rebellion against self-proclaimed "authorities." If you felt you had to do the opposite of whatever they told you, your actions would still be controlled, albeit in a perverse way, by their commands. To go your own way is to listen and decide for yourself, whether you wind up agreeing or disagreeing with others' advice.

This point is made strikingly by the clear allusion to the closing doxology of the Lord's Prayer ("For thine is the kingdom, and the power, and the glory, forever. Amen"). Here these phrases are reapplied: you are to seek your own kingdom, your own glory, your own power, your own story. Compare this paraphrase with that in "The

Weapon," which mocks the glory game, the power train, the kingdom of fear whose will is done. The two songs are, so to speak, praying the Lord's Prayer in different directions. "The Weapon" uses it as a sarcastic poem to the self-aggrandizing power of the wielders of fear, the religious (and other) authorities who, like Dostoevsky's Grand Inquisitor, enslave us through our own fears and insecurities. We willingly hand them the keys to our own safe and secure prison cells. We pray to them with grateful submissiveness.

By contrast, in "Something for Nothing," the prayer is directed to one's own soul, one's own sense of destiny, purpose, and selfhood. What we have here, in the terms used so illuminatingly by Kant and Tillich, is the contrast between *heteronomous* and *autonomous* existence. In other words, will you take your direction from the law (*nomos*) as laid down for you by others (*heteroi*) or from the law of your own (*autos*) being?

"The Big Money"

The very same contrast appears when we compare "Something for Nothing" with "The Big Money," for here, too, we find a paraphrase of the Lord's Prayer's doxology: we hear of the power and the glory, the kingdom Big Money would rule. This time, worship is being directed to The Big Money. Let's pursue the religious imagery which is actually quite central to the song.

In Jesus's day, "Mammon" was a name denoting money worshiped as a god. We say the same thing with the phrase "the Almighty Dollar." Jesus says "You cannot serve both God and Mammon" (Matthew 6:24, just across the page from "For thine is the kingdom, and the power, and the glory, forever. Amen." (Matthew 6:13). "The Big Money" is a song about Mammon-worship, the old-time religion and the kingdom it would rule. Here we are meant to think back to a few lines to when we heard of the power and the glory, a war in paradise. That is the mythical war hinted at in Revelations 12:7-9 and chronicled by Milton, the war between God and Satan, who sought to usurp the heavenly throne. He lost and was cast down to earth, where he ruled by dazzling men and women with the wealth of kingdoms:

> And the devil, taking him up to a high mountain, showed him all the *kingdoms* of the world in a moment of time. And the devil said to him, "All this *power* will I give you, and the *glory* of them; for it is delivered unto me, and to whomsoever I will, I give it. If you, therefore, will worship me, all shall be yours." (Luke 4:5-7)

There is our familiar triad: kingdoms, power, glory.

85

Another possible image suggesting that The Big Money is devilish is the suggestion that it weaves a mighty web, it draws the flies. Besides being an obvious image for the seductive lure of wealth, this is also a reference to the ancient Jewish title for the devil, "Beelzebub" (Mark 3:22), which means "Lord of the Flies." His unwitting worship by those who barter their souls (sacrifice their moral values) for material wealth is indeed an old-time religion, perhaps the oldest.

That old-time religion, however, might also refer to the disgusting record of established religion which worships Mammon even as it hypocritically condemns him. (More hypocrites slandering the sacred halls of truth.) Nowhere is this disgrace more flagrant than on religious television, where disproportionate amounts of airtime are consumed wheedling contributions from viewers so that God's favorite show can stay on the air, grabbing those Nielson ratings of salvation as new converts and, more importantly, new contributors, phone into the show's switchboard. And why stay on the air, pray tell? What do they plan to do with the air time? Why, cajole more money, of course! And who knows how much is going from the offering plate into the TV evangelist's pocket? Only God knows, that is, if he ever bothers to tune in, though somehow that's hard to imagine.

But Mammon as a godlike Power is certainly the focus in the song. Listen to the attributes of the Almighty Dollar as they are chanted off, as in a litany: it goes around the world. It is all embracing; nothing escapes its tentacles. As the network president informs Howard Beale, the Mad Prophet of the Airwaves in Paddy Chayefsky's film *Network,* political divisions are purely cosmetic. The world works on the ebb and flow of the international economy. American finance pros are just as concerned about dips in Japan's Nikkei Stock Exchange as they are about what happens on Wall Street. How's the dollar doing against other world currencies? What's the current picture on the international balance of trade? All of this matters because, though there may be many countries, there is one world market.

Yet for all its globe-girdling girth, Big Money exercises its power underground. No one wants to admit the extent to which the unelected bosses of multinational corporations, not elected government officials, set foreign policy. Certainly government officials don't want to admit how easily influenced they are by commercial interests and lobbies which buy their votes on relevant issues by making big contributions to campaign funds.

Big Money has a mighty voice, yet it makes no sound. In fact, the more silent it is, the mightier it is, since no one will think to fight what they do not suspect exists!

Big Money has a heavy hand; it quickly takes control. Big Money has a mean streak instead of a soul. These are certainly harsh words! Why is big business so indifferent toward people that it is happy to throw them out like so much garbage when some new technology makes their jobs superfluous? Or when cheaper labor may be hired in a Third World country? Why are big corporations heedless of environmental damage? Why did one company promote the use of infant formula in underdeveloped countries where contaminated water made it dangerous, all the while telling uneducated mothers that the stuff was better than mothers' milk? Is it that business is controlled, by a bitter accident, by so many dollar-loving, people-hating Scrooges and Marleys? No, that would be a caricature. Is it that business corrupts people who were humane when they began? It's not so simple as that, either. Rather, it is the logic of *efficiency*, the great commandment of business.

For business the world is a machine, one great assembly line. Employees are simply part of that mechanism. What care is taken of them on the advice of "industrial psychologists" is taken not for the sake of the workers, but rather for greater efficiency's sake. Happier workers make more widgets per hour, so let's make them as happy as we have to, as long as it doesn't cost as much as the extra widgets would sell for! (As Homer Simpson's boss once said, grudgingly granting an employee wish: "Let the fools have their tartar sauce!") And by all means, let's use machines instead of workers if their maintenance contracts are cheaper than employee health plans. (We don't feed the people, but we feed the machines; in fact sometimes we even feed the people *to* the machines in the case of weapons-technology!)

It's simply the mass-production zone all over again: human beings are viewed under the Big Money system merely as *producers*. Insofar as they produce efficiently they are valued as good. Why do you suppose companies are suddenly interested in promoting employee health, in offering programs to help you quit smoking and lose weight, in administering drug tests?

Simply because they get a greater return on their investment from a healthier worker. And this is true even when the company is dedicated to producing products that will destroy the health of individuals or the environment.

Big Money funds public television and charitable organizations. Tobacco companies fund the arts, sporting events, and celebrations of the Bill of Rights. *Playboy* contributes to Women's Liberation causes. All this, however much their own *raisons d'être* mitigate against these things. These operations are exercises in covering your tracks, in erecting camouflage screens. Sometimes Big Money pushes all the buttons, but other times it pulls out the plug. Sometimes it builds ivory towers, but other times it knocks castles down. Sometimes it seems to build you a stairway, but it winds up taking you underground. Though it may have done a powerful bit of good, it will bury you when your usefulness as a producer and/or consumer is over.

87

Ours is a Capitalist society. Everything is predicated on everyone doing their bit to spend money, to buy each other's services. As Aristotle said, that much is probably basic to any society. But modern Capitalism is Capitalism run riot. You are unpatriotic if you don't buy your quota of junk. It's someone's job to make those pet rocks and superfluous "Baby on Board" car-window signs, so if you don't buy them, you're putting that poor schmuck out of work! Just as if you lived in Bolivia or Afghanistan, you might be considered unpatriotic if you were against drug use!

With Supercapitalism, advertising, too, has run riot. Now all public discourse is advertising, and all advertising, in turn, is a lot of hype without facts. Advertisements make up an annoyingly huge percentage of any magazine's or newspaper's pages. Landscapes are marred by endless obnoxious billboards. It is as if someone spray-painted EAT AT JOE'S across the Mona Lisa. It would sure get your attention!

Ads strive to generate feelings and to associate them, arbitrarily, with products. Somehow Wrigley's Gum is to be associated with "strapping your snowboard on" and zooming down the slope. Somehow Marlboro is to be associated with he-man cowboys instead of sniveling pimple-faced adolescents trying to assert their illusory manhood. "Can't stop the feeling!"—are they advertising Coca-Cola or Cocaine? And how is the "Pepsi Generation" distinctive from other generations? Is it perhaps more gullible?

Since such ads prove so effective, politicians (who want to gull and con the public whenever they can) have seized on the slogan, the sound-bite, the feel-good commercial to lull the public into voting for them, or at least into not impeaching or overthrowing the rascals. Political discourse is now nothing but propaganda. A candidate's speech or debate performance is evaluated solely on the basis of how effective it was in pushing up his standing in the polls: marketing, pure and simple.

Television and movies are nothing but strings of overt or covert commercials. As Gahan Wilson once pointed out, the movie *Gremlins* was little more than a two-hour commercial for the sickeningly cute little "Gizmo" dolls timed to fill toy store shelves in time for Christmas. Cartoons like *He-Man* or the nauseatingly saccharine "Care-Bears" are nothing but commercials for toys. Notice how in *Superman II* the big fight-scene between Superman and his Kryptonian foes was just the vehicle to promote the various brand names emblazoned on billboards and buses which the villains smashed. *E.T.* was just a two-hour ad for Reece's Pieces.

All commercial TV is TV commercials. "News" is tailored to fit the minute attention span created by years of commercial-watching. TV series are insipid because the producers want to risk offending nobody, so they systematically lower viewing standards to a lowest common denominator. They copy each other if one network happens upon a hit show. And if a series doesn't get good ratings in a week, it is canned. American media is dedicated in all of its forms to sell the stuff promoted in the ever-present commercials. This must be why the cult of the media celebrity has risen so high that the latest divorce of some Hollywood prostitute is considered as newsworthy, fully as important as the invasion of a country or a natural disaster. Shows like *Good Morning America* imply that Suzy Starlett talking about how she likes her co-stars on the set is as important as an interview with Henry Kissinger about Middle East tensions. If we can be convinced that these things are on the same level, and we have been, then we will believe that watching idiotic sitcoms and soap operas is a worthwhile thing to spend dozens of hours a week doing—and soaking up those commercials, and buying those products, of course!

It is no wonder that as soon as religion joined up with Big Money it became corrupt. It had perforce to drop the unpleasant side of its gospel—that God requires self-sacrifice for the good of others and discipline for one's own good. That kind of thing just doesn't get good ratings! People want to feel good, so they will tune in to the kind of religion that tells them God will make them rich, that they will have no problems, that God will heal them. All integrity vanishes like the picture when you switch off the tube (something Americans never seem to do!). What TV evangelists have done is to contract with Mammon: they can have glitzy TV studios and programs if they will only preach Mammon's gospel. Quite simply, they're the fools on television getting paid to play the fool.

But it is not only TV preachers who have to reckon with such temptations. In ways great and small, every individual has to decide what is at stake in every deal offered by Big Money. If an avenue of success seems to be opening before you, what will it cost you to take it? Is the price your moral or artistic integrity? Will you have to compromise your standards? Will you have to betray your artistic vision? Will you jettison your sense of personal destiny, ditch any sense of mission and responsibility to your world, like most college students surveyed seem willing to do, if that's the only way to guarantee yourself a nice fat check?

Big Money can pull a million strings because Big Money holds the prize. Big Money spins a mighty web to draw the flies. Will you be one of them? Lured by the dangled prospect of a good job, will you sacrifice authenticity for a few extra bucks? Will you heedlessly walk into that web? If you do, you will find yourself trapped by the surprisingly strong adhesive of money. Soon, like a hollow insect skeleton, you will find yourself sucked dry by Big Money. Big Money has no soul, and you won't either.

Finally, we see the stark contrast between "Something for Nothing" and "The Big Money." Both titles, both songs, use mercantile imagery. You might even say that the listener addressed in "Something for Nothing," waiting and waiting for someone else to come and solve his problems, is hoping to be "discovered" and seduced by Big Money. On its own terms "Something for Nothing" is telling you your dreams won't be realized for free. But "The Big Money" adds to that picture the warning that you can pay too *much* for the realization of your dreams (Big Money has a million dreams), namely *your soul.* Being a sold-out phony is hardly better than being a lazy zero. Why choose either one, when by safeguarding your own integrity you can follow your dreams in a path you select. There may not be as much profit or reward if you do it that way, but that's only if material goodies are all you think of as profit and reward. As in *Citizen Kane,* "There's no trick to making money, if all you want to do is make money." If that is all you want to do, your destiny is to be one more drone, one more cog, one more Digital Man. Poor Schmuck.

"The Spirit of Radio"

It is against the admittedly pessimistic background of "The Big Money" that "The Spirit of Radio" (*Permanent Waves,* 1980) must be seen if we are to understand it rightly. Otherwise, the first few stanzas of the song sound deceptively innocent, and the second half seems to be an abrupt, even arbitrary, reversal: you begin the day innocently enough with a friendly voice, an unobtrusive companion, your radio, which plays a song that's so elusive. The disembodied sound sets the mood as you're on your way. There is magic at your fingertips in the dashboard radio tuner. The spirit of radio hovers about you, lingers, seeming to make no demands of you, leaving you in a bubble of reverie. But it does carry a price tag. Like Rumplestiltskin or Mephistopheles it will sooner or later come to collect.

There are clues even here, before the mask falls in the next stanzas, that all is not what it seems. Remember, you do not live in neutral territory. You live in the Mass-Production Zone, a world ruled by Big Money. Every bit of entertainment is geared to make you buy, to help you fulfill your patriotic duty as a passive consumer. The radio, with the pleasantly vacuous banter of morning show hosts, is a seemingly "unobtrusive companion," but it is the everpresent voice of Big Money, like *Nineteen Eighty-Four*'s Big Brother, always urging you to buy. Every song is a commercial for a record as well as being a siren voice to keep you listening through the endless minutes of ads till the next song. The songs are window dressing for the ads, sugar to help you swallow the medicine. They are no more, really, than the piped-in Muzak in a supermarket or department store. Industrial psychologists tell us that such music will lull the shopper, incline him to

buy more. As Malcolm Muggeridge called it, the output of the car radio is a continuous stream of alternating Muzak and "newzak."
   Is the spirit of radio truly so undemanding after all? No, it is
the sweet-voiced propaganda of Big Brother constantly brainwashing
and programming you to BUY BUY BUY! When you get to work,
your office mates will already have another radio on, and on it will stay
all day. At the bar after work, a radio or TV will spew forth more
commercial propaganda, and when you get home, you will of course
turn on the TV. You will even keep the set on when you leave the
room, as if it were a guest you would be rude to throw out. You are
part of a generation raised within constant earshot of the idiot box.
Without its ubiquitous background noise, you would feel disturbed.
Better to turn on the set. Even if you talk or read and don't actually
listen (*though why the hell would you have it on if not to watch or listen?* Do you see how thoroughly you are programmed?), the message is
getting through—like one of those subliminal sleep-learning cassettes.
   So much for solitude. You are never without the noise of
mind-disintegrating pop radio or TV. It is like the cosmic three-degree
radiation left over from the Big Bang; it echoes unnoticed through your
universe. That TV set, that radio, is just like the two-way screen in
Winston Smith's apartment in Orwell's *Nineteen Eighty-Four.* Of
course, no one is actually peering out at you through your TV screen
(unless you are a "Nielson family"!), but the Network and the sponsors
are keeping their eye on you right enough, since they've seduced you
into watching, always watching, their swill.
   That gift is almost free, but not quite. Commercial radio and
TV are like the Trojan Horse. You are welcoming your conquerors
into the city walls.
   In the rest of the song, Rush addresses the complicity of musicians who have sold out to Big Money to sing the anthems of the Mass-
Production Zone. They write and sing what will sell, what is just like
what already sells. So much of modern music, so heavily mechanized,
might as well have been composed by machine as well! It is formula-
fodder driven not by the Muse but by market forces. This accounts for
the cranked-out character of so much music. Your Whitney Houstons,
your Barry Manilows, your Madonnas, your Guns 'N Roses, your Poisons, your Motley Crües, your Elvis impersonator impersonators. This
Muzak simply embodies the same tried-and-true tripe, the same insipid
formula pop, whether schmaltz or heavy-metal. Record companies
know which buttons to push to elicit the required schoolgirl maudlin
sentimentality, the same pre-teen leather-jacket pseudo-rebellious swagger described so well in "Superconductor."
   George Orwell anticipated all this in *Nineteen Eighty-Four,* his
prophetic novel of manipulative totalitarian society written back in
1949. In one scene Winston Smith, disillusioned party hack, is looking
out the window and spies a lower-class housewife (one of the "proles"

or proletarians, the Marxist term for the lowly workers) singing in her Cockney contralto, as she hangs diapers out to dry. "It was only an 'opeless fancy / It passed like an Ipril dye / But a look an' a word an' the dreams they stirred / They 'ave stolen my 'eart awye!" The narrator reflects,

> The tune had been haunting London for weeks past. It was one of countless similar songs published for the benefit of the proles by a sub-section of the Music Department. The words of these songs were composed without any human intervention whatever on an instrument known as a versificator.

There's your machinery making modern music, coldly chanted!

What sort of stuff gets recorded? As far as the music industry is concerned, it's strictly Target: Mass Appeal ("Superconductor"). Note the blasphemous mockery of Simon and Garfunkel's 1960s folk song about the roots of art in the suffering of the downtrodden. The original speaks of the inspired words of the prophets inscribed on subway walls ("that he may run that readeth it"—Habakkuk 2:2.) and in tenement halls, which echo with the sounds of silence. Rush indicts today's commercial music scene as writing words of the *profits*, on the recording studio wall, in concert halls that echo with the sounds of salesmen.

Recent years have witnessed a debate over whether there can be "pure science" when labs are funded by industry and the military. Good question! Won't the results be tainted? Won't only profitable medicines and inventions be developed? Rush is raising the same question about the music industry. Can the integrity of the artist survive when producers clamor for "what sells?" (Big Money just might pull out the plug!) It would be nice to believe in the freedom of music, but all the glittering prizes and endless compromises finally destroy any illusion of integrity. Do you need examples? Trace the slow decline of Jefferson Airplane to "Starship." Compare the music of the two incarnations of the group. Or chart the precipitous sell-out of the Sex Pistols. Their bitter, nihilistic songs excoriated a Britain whose economy cancelled any viable future for the Kingdom's youth, but somehow these lyrics rang hollow when the group signed with Big Money and became a "kept band" in principle no different from the Partridge Family. The music may have sounded pretty much the same as it had before, but it stank with hypocrisy and became merely "fashionable pessimism," "radical chic." The illusion of integrity had been shattered. Sid Vicious and Johnny Rotten were packaged like rebels or heroes to con the audience into feeling they really meant what they sang (see "Superconductor").

Yet you need not give in. One need not sell out. Big Money underestimates the taste of the public (though, as someone has said, no one ever lost money doing this!). As the Music Department underestimates listener tastes, they make a self-fulfilling prophecy. The versificator will crank out more drivel and hokum, and people *will* listen to it and buy it. But they *might* be even happier to pay for a better product if it were available. Why think music with integrity wouldn't sell? Popular music can still be open-hearted if you want it to be. It's finally a question of honesty.

Every page of the present book is implicitly an argument that Rush managed to make it big without selling out. The hackneyed themes of teen love, mindless hedonism, and adolescent swaggering are conspicuous by their absence. How many groups try to defy the market trend and sing songs about philosophy, motivation, paradox, and integrity? Sadly, not many, but the success of Rush indicates that the proles might buy more than drivel if more were available.

"2112"

"Something for Nothing" is, as we have seen, about personal initiative as the only road to fulfilling one's dreams and guarding one's integrity. The song ends with the metaphor of one's own song as one's authentic personal path. In "The Spirit of Radio," we saw how the integrity of a musician can be tempted and seduced by the Big Money music industry, where all becomes mere marketing campaigns (as in "Natural Science"), no longer real art. We close the circle with our discussion of "2112," a song, or cycle of songs, in which music is used metonymously as a symbol for individual integrity and excellence above and beyond the tide of mediocrity in the Mass-Production Zone.

The song begins with two tips of the hat to its inspirations. The title, "2112," denotes the date of the futuristic dystopia in which the song's action takes place. The title—simply the date—is perhaps intended to recall Arthur C. Clarke's movie *2001*, but whereas that film promoted a cosmic optimism about humanity's future, "2112" rings with bitter pessimism, or at least with warning signals about what could come to pass if we as a civilization are not careful.

Why the choice of this *particular* date? Notice that the first piece of music in the set is the "Overture." The "2112" "Overture" is, then, an updating of Tchaikovsky's famous *1812 Overture* written to commemorate the War of 1812.

More important to the meaning of the song is the opening "acknowledgment to the genius of Ayn Rand." Rand, an expatriate Russian philosopher-novelist, was an archconservative anti-communist. In works like the nonfiction *The Virtue of Selfishness* and the novel *The Fountainhead*, she extolled the value of the creative, autonomous individual over against the stifling, leveling power of the mediocre "collectivity." No doubt she was initially horrified at the excesses of Stalinism in the Soviet Union. There the party line of Socialism and anti-elitism conjured a collectivist nightmare. Party dogma controlled thought and squelched art. History was rewritten, and any historical studies which questioned the "official" version of the past were censored. Philosophy's wings were clipped. Philosophical inquiry demands freedom of thought with no bounds, but the State prescribed careful limits within which Soviet philosophers might safely theorize (*i.e.*, those laid down by Marx and Engels, whose theories, ironically, *were* the products of free and daring intellects!).

In the field of science, Darwinism was thought to be anti-Socialist. Inherently elitist, involving as it did the belief that species evolve when gifted members of a species arise, excel, and dominate their species. In nineteenth-century America, Darwinism had in fact become a ruthless socio-economic doctrine, "Social Darwinism": if only the fittest are destined to survive, then we need not waste time and money on the poor or infirm. "Let them die and decrease the surplus population!," as Ebenezer Scrooge ranted. In overreaction to this cruel philosophy, Soviet planners rejected the biological Darwinism that had led to it, and Lysenko, the director of Soviet agronomy, engineered State agricultural policy in line with the scientifically discredited but ideologically congenial theory of Lamarck, which held that the environment caused mutation and species adaptation. To shorten a long story, this disastrous plan, the product of inflexible ideology, resulted in a ruined wheat harvest. Thousands starved.

Ideological purity, pursued with a zeal equal to the Spanish Inquisition, flattened and censored every aspect of Soviet society. The arts did not escape the scrutiny of the ideologues. Rand, George Orwell, and others were horrified to witness the birth of something called "Socialist Realism" in the visual art media. Clean-lined and big-boned statues and paintings of Soviet workers and peasants sprouted all over the landscape. Art had become propaganda, pure and simple. Drama, poetry, fiction, dance, and music all had to pass the test of ideological purity. And if the Soviet counterparts of Siskel and Ebert didn't grant you a "thumbs-up," you wound up in a little artists' colony called the Gulag. You can see where Orwell got the idea for the Ministry of Truth.

Economically, the Soviet policy was collectivization. Private ownership of business and agriculture was abolished. Workers were herded into state-run farms and factories. The Marxist dogma was: "From each according to his ability, to each according to his need." The idea was to avoid the outrage of wealthy industrial barons and agribusiness tycoons making piles of money through the cheap labor of exploited workers. Marxism sought to equalize things. You, the worker, ought to do your best for the good of all. You, the individual, would not enjoy direct profit from your extra labor, but the level of *general* prosperity would rise by that much more. You would benefit, but several stages down the line. The problem is that, given human nature, such a system does not reward anyone enough, or quickly enough, to make any extra effort seem worthwhile. Everybody gets an equal share of the pie, but the pie does not seem to get any bigger. There are more mouths to get a share, and everyone's share is smaller. It gets smaller still when you come to conclude that you are just wasting your efforts and decide not to bother doing more than your job—if that. Witness the economic chaos of *every single* Communist region!

There was plenty of reason to be an anti-Communist, but Rand was more than that. The "Soviet Experiment" was for her a rude shock awakening her to the danger that lurked in *every* society where collectivism reared its head, under whatever name. Rand tried to wake people up to the dangers of the same poison in America, too. Have you ever wondered how Communist (or once-Communist) states could call themselves things like "The German Democratic Republic" (East Germany) or the "Democratic Republic of Korea" (North Korea)? Isn't it a cruel, even sarcastic, joke to call such a regime "democratic?" C. S. Lewis explained the infernal logic behind such nomenclature. He said that such a use of the word is

> purely as an incantation;...purely for its selling power.... And of course it is connected with the political ideal that men should be equally treated. You then make a stealthy transition...from this political ideal to a factual belief that all men *are* equal.... As a result you can use the word *Democracy* to sanction... the most degrading...of all human feelings... This feeling I mean is of course that which prompts a man to say *I'm as good as you*... No man who says *I'm as good as you* believes it. He would not say it if he did. The St. Bernard never says it to the toy dog, nor the scholar to the dunce, nor the employable to the bum, nor the pretty woman to the plain. The claim to equality, outside the strictly political field, is made only by those who feel themselves to be in some way inferior. What it expresses is precisely the itching, smarting, writhing awareness of an inferiority which [one] refuses to accept. [Therefore he] resents every kind of superiority in others; denigrates it; wishes its annihilation. Presently he suspects every mere difference of being a claim to superiority. No one must be different from himself in voice, clothes, manners, recreations, choice of food... "If they were the right sort of chaps, they'd be like me. They've no business to be different. It's undemocratic." [By using

"democracy" as their excuse, such people will] labour more whole-heartedly and successfully than ever before to pull everyone else to their own level.

(C. S. Lewis, "Screwtape Proposes a Toast")

"The Trees"

Rush has another clearly Rand-inspired song, "The Trees" (*Hemispheres*, 1978). This seems perhaps the best place to give it some brief discussion. The song depicts a dispute between the shorter Maples and the towering Oaks. The Maple gripe is this: the Oaks are too tall! They hog all the light! But who can blame the Oaks for being proud of their height? Perhaps a bit smugly they wonder why the Maples can't be happy in their shade. The Maples scream "Oppression!" The Oaks, befuddled, just shake their heads. The Maples get organized and demand equal rights. The solution? Oak ascendancy is over, thanks to a just decree. All trees henceforth are chopped down to equality. The Lowest Common Denominator becomes the rule. The Maples, of course, are those who mutter "I'm as good as you!" and who hobble their superiors to make it so in truth!

Lewis goes on to use almost precisely the same analogy, when he recalls the political philosophy of one of the ancient Greek Tyrants. He

> led the envoy into a field of corn, and there he snicked off with his cane the top of every stalk that rose an inch or so above the general level. The moral was plain. Allow no pre-eminence among your subjects. Let no man live who is wiser, or better, or more famous, or even handsomer than the mass. Cut them all down to a level; all slaves, all ciphers, all nobodies. All equals. Thus Tyrants could practise, in a sense, "democracy." But now "democracy" can do the same work without any other tyranny than her own. No one need now go through the field with a cane. The little stalks will now of themselves bite the tops off the big ones.
>
> ("Screwtape Proposes a Toast")

(One cannot help but recall Lysenko's anti-Darwin wheat harvest—he was taking the ancient Tyrant's advice literally!)

Just as Lewis saw such tendencies operative in England, so Rand saw them gaining ground in her adopted homeland, America. She wrote to expose them. She saw that art and individuality are impossible in a society that makes mediocrity *normative* instead of merely *normal*. When mediocrity becomes the ruling principle in a society, we have *mediocracy*. When, as "2112" says in its opening line, "The meek shall inherit the earth," excellence becomes blasphemy, because it is a stinging and intolerable reminder that the mass cannot excel.

Here Rand parallels Heidegger and Nietzsche, both of whom lamented the stifling coma-existence one experiences in "the herd," among one's fellow cowards and slaves (Nietzsche), as part of *"das Mann"* and his "inauthentic existence" (Heidegger).

"2112" pictures such a "mediocracy," an Orwellian state in a future time. The meek rule, because the elder race of man has long since departed to seek its glorious destiny in the stars, leaving behind what Lovecraft called "the self-blinded earth-gazers" who have no dream but to squelch every vestige of excellence and individualism. The mass of the meek are ruled by a group of elite priests. These theocratic hierarchs are clones of Dostoyevsky's Grand Inquisitor, guardians of a religion of "comfortable numbness," according to which all thought, all decision, all responsibility, have been gratefully traded to the warden for security, shelter under the gun. Like the Grand Inquisitor, these priests have distorted the words of Jesus to serve their ends. "And the meek shall inherit the earth" comes from a kind of Orwellian Newspeak version of the New Testament in which Jesus pronounces, "Blessed are the meek for they shall inherit the earth" (Matthew 5:5). Gone is any memory of the original context in which the statement flamed like a populist beacon in the darkness of oppression, a challenge to the aristocratic rule of the wealthy, status-quo worshipping Sadducees, Lords of the Jerusalem Temple—dead ringers, in fact for the priests of the Temples of Syrinx in "2112!"

Nietzsche, too, realized that Jesus, whom he viewed as a Promethean Übermensch, had been recreated in the image of the cringing cowards who came to follow him and blasphemously invoked his noble name as an excuse for their surrender. In the same way, we may view the narrator/singer in "2112" as a kind of Christ-figure martyr, even though he opposes a religious establishment. In fact, it is perhaps ironic that the closest parallels in popular music and verse to "2112," a song dedicated to Rand, a militant atheist, are by Christian artists. These are Ken Medema's song, "You Can't Go Back" (1974), and Calvin Miller's blank-verse poem, *The Singer* (1975). In fact, so close are the three works in theme and imagery that they seem to supplement and fill gaps in each other's picture. Julia Kristeva would say they are "intertextual" with each other.

"2112" opens by setting the stage, as we have seen, by announcing that the meek, the mediocre, Nietzsche's slaves and cowards, have inherited the earth. Not *seized* it, mind you, as that would have required courage and initiative that they lack. No, the earth passed to them by default when the most venturesome elements of humanity blasted off for the stars (as we learn in Section V, "Oracle: The Dream").

The resulting society is a totalitarian prison, though so anesthetized are the comatose inmates that they do not even realize their true condition. One of them muses how he has always stood in awe of the Temples of Syrinx, marveling that every facet of every life should be regulated and directed from inside. All ideas, pursuits, even all music is prescribed by the benevolent wisdom of the priests. The loyal prisoner is a victim of false consciousness, an android in the Mass-Production Zone, who is soon to become a humanoid escapee.

The looming fortress walls of Syrinx rise in the midst of each Federation city, very much like the four massive white concrete pyramids rising above the London skyline in Orwell's *Nineteen Eighty-Four*:

> They were the homes of the four Ministries between which the entire apparatus of government was divided: the Ministry of Truth, which concerned itself with news, entertainment, education and the fine arts; the Ministry of Peace, which concerned itself with war; the Ministry of Love, which maintained law and order; and the Ministry of Plenty, which was responsible for economic affairs.

We have essentially the same scene in "2112," albeit "The Federation" is probably a poor choice of name, since it reminds the listener incongruously of the optimistic, humanistic *Star Trek*, contrary to the gloomy feel of the rest of the song, which invokes the pessimistic futures of *Nineteen Eighty-Four* and *Brave New World*.

In Miller's *The Singer*, the priests' counterparts are "the Keepers of the Ancient Ways. They were every one gray-bearded and wore pointed hats, the custom of their ordered service at the shrine. Each sang the hymns of their tradition and kept with strict obedience the rituals of the ages" (XVI). The Lords of Syrinx announce themselves grandiosely as the priests of the Temples of Syrinx, whose great computers fill the hallowed halls. All life's gifts are safely stockpiled there. Medema's hierarchs speak with tones similarly redolent of an iron fist in a velvet glove: They are the lords of the land of *Ecclesia* (Greek for "church"). They alone hold the key to Eternity's door. They keep the fortresses; they've got the treasuries. Those in this flock, they promise soothingly, will be safe evermore.

It is such promises of safety and security that the priests have used to lord it over the consciences of their subjects. Medema's Lords of Ecclesia invite them to come and hear the soothing words, listen to the promises. Those in the sheep-like flock will be safe evermore. Rush's priests of Syrinx announce, in exactly the same vein, that they've made equality their stock in trade. They invite the hearer, who really has no choice in the matter, to come and join the Brotherhood of

Man. In such a nice contented world no one ever troubles his head with questions again.

The placid pond of dreaming totalitarianism is briefly troubled once the narrator discovers a dusty old guitar hidden in a cave. He does not even know what it is; such instruments have long ago been destroyed. The authorities considered them too dangerous; best not to risk enflaming hearts and dreams with songs of love and freedom. But of all this the narrator as yet suspects nothing. He teaches himself how to play the instrument, as the inventor of the lute did thousands of years ago.

Miller's Singer, too, has a moment of fateful discovery:

> When he awoke, the song was there.
> Its melody beckoned and begged him to sing it.
> It hung upon the wind and settled in the meadows
> where he walked.
> He knew its lovely words and could have sung it
> all, but feared to sing a song whose harmony was far
> too perfect for human ear to understand.
> And still at midnight it stirred him to awareness,
> and with its haunting melody it drew him with a curi-
> ous mystery to stand before an open window.
> In rhapsody it played among the stars.
> It rippled through Andromeda and deepened
> Vega's hues.
> It swirled in heavy strains from galaxy to galaxy
> and gave him back his fingerprint.
> "Sing the Song!" the heavens seemed to cry.
> "We never could have been without the melody that
> you alone can sing."

The rediscoverer of ancient music resolves to take it to the priests for an audition. But he receives, to say the least, a chilly reception. Rush's liner notes summarize the confrontation: The priests greet his recital with stony silence. Then Father Brown (a grossly anticlimactic name, it must be admitted, for a dystopian Antichrist such as Peart intends!) speaks quiet words that nonetheless somehow manage to echo through the whole temple (an example of the half-thought-through character of the writing which mars the song). His verdict: this performance is not destined for the Hit Parade. Like John Belushi in *Animal House*, the wicked priest puts an end to the heresy by smashing the offending guitar to splinters.

The Singer meets a similar fate, but unlike Rush's narrator, he had expected it:

Full well he knew that few would ever see him as a singer of so grand a piece.

He knew that they would say to him:

'You are no singer! And even if you are you should sing the songs we know.'

And well he knew the penalty of law. A dreamer could be ostracized in hate for singing songs the world had never heard.

Such songs had sent a thousand singers to their death already.

And the song which dogged his aching steps and begged him pleadingly to sing it was completely unfamiliar.

Only the stars and mountains knew it. But they were old. And man was new, and chained to simple, useless rhymes....

At length the Singer does encounter the Keepers of the Ancient Ways.

The Singer took his lyre and strummed the strings. The chords fell outward over all the throng.

The audience grew still.... Above him towered the wall and high upon the bulwark he saw the framework of a strange machine. It was the great machine on which false singers met their death.

He knew then what it meant to sing a new song.

And then his finger swept the strings and he began the final verse.

The result?

"And now I pass the sentence. We shall break his lyre, then we shall break his hand and set him free. On the flesh of his forehead we shall burn the word 'Liar' and he shall live beneath his sentence all his life."

Both hands are broken and at last he is condemned to death upon the Wall.

Though the Keepers disdain "new songs," it is clear that the Singer brought to their hearing the primordial Song of creation that established the world itself. But it is new because so long unheard. It is unwelcome because, once heard, it might create again, and if it did, the carefully designed world of their own making would crumble to make way for the renewal. This they cannot risk. The Singer is a "false singer" only because he is not "true" to their illusion. "2112" envisions precisely the same paradox. The priests of Syrinx hear the guitarist's music and dismiss it as nothing more than stale heresy, more of the old passion that helped destroy the elder race of man. They have no need for outmoded ancient ways.

At first glance, the Syrinx priests appear to reject what the Keepers uphold, ancient ways. But the contrast is illusory. The Singer's Song was more ancient than the ways safeguarded by the Keepers. And both groups of clerics fear exactly the same thing: the reintroduction of an ancient force of *renewal* that is destructive only in its threat to their perverted order. The Syrinx priests either purposely distort or fail to understand the relation of the old music to the fate of the elder race of man. Perhaps all they know of the elder race's absence is the fact of it, not the reason for it. They know the "ancients" (2112 is only one hundred thirty-six years away from the date of this album!) are gone and that the music had something to do with it, so they suppose that the music helped to destroy them. In fact, as the oracle implies later, the music helped fuel the dreams that sent humanity rocketing skyward (as in "Countdown"). The old music is not dangerous because it destroyed the *old* world; it *didn't*. But it is indeed dangerous to the priests, since it has the potential to destroy *their* "brave, new world."

The disillusioned narrator of "2112" retreats into dreams which reveal the wonder of the vanished world of which his late, lamented guitar was a lone relic. Though he abandons himself to suicidal despair, he seems to envision a hopeful future. What *is* the prospect glimpsed on the horizon in "2112?" The dream-oracle reveals that the elder human race who left the planet long ago may one day return and claim the home where they belong. They may arrive in time to tear the Temples down.

Medema supplies more of the vision, graphically depicting the impotent terror of the Lords of Ecclesia on the day that the renewing music sweeps clean. Their cherished yester-music will be a dull sword in the day of battle, he sings as he envisions the panic of the Lords. They hear the wind sweeping like wildfire across the land, breaking down the ancient statues. They try to stop it but they just cannot understand. In stunned silence they witness the dissolution. They rush for safety but find it not. Within the walls of the fortress confusion reigns, their mighty castles being burned slowly to the ground.

Though the narrator of "2112" himself seems to despair, that is not the last word on the matter. The front inside and outside covers of the *2112* album depict features from the song. Both picture a red star in a red circle. Though some may jump to the conclusion that what is shown here is the Satanic pentangle, it cannot be, since the Satanic star points *down,* not up. Rather, the symbol is the official emblem of Syrinx: unfurled banners sport the Red Star as a proud ensign. The lone figure standing before the star on the inside cover is not a conjurer in a pentacle, but rather the narrator of the song recoiling against the intimidation of the priests. His posture denotes he is trying to keep their threats, their dooms, away.

The Red Star has become a trademark symbol for Rush, emblazoning posters and shirts. Why? It is a constant reminder of the danger and challenge of what the Red Star represents in "2112." It is a gauntlet thrown down against the sapping, vitiating, compromising influence of Big Money, the Mass-Production Zone, the priests of Syrinx. It is a clenching plastic fist raised in defiance, a vow to maintain artistic integrity amid today's music scene where the most popular products are cranked out by the computers of Syrinx, written without human inspiration in the Music Department of the Ministry of Truth.

VI.

THE FABRIC OF THEIR DREAMS

One of Rush's recurrent themes is that of dreams, of hope. It is not that the idea comes up all that often or in most of their songs; they have too much to sing about for any one theme to predominate to that degree. But one need not try very hard to notice how the theme of dreams, hopes, and aspirations occurs quietly and unobtrusively again and again over the years in Rush's body of lyrics.

In this chapter I want to survey some of the more important songs dealing with dreams and the strength they impart to the struggling soul. A handy organizing principle will be to ask, for each song, just what are dreams *opposed* to? What is hope the *alternative* to? This way, we may be able to approach the subject from several of the various perspectives contained in the lyrics.

"Jacob's Ladder"

"Jacob's Ladder" (*Permanent Waves*, 1980) serves as the signpost, pointing the direction for all the dream songs. It provides the basic image of dreams as our *vision of possibility*. On the face of it, the short song is simply a description of one of those wonderful moments when the dense clouds begin to part after a rainy, overcast day, making a hole in the celestial dike that allows a narrow shaft of blindingly pure sunlight to break through.

That lone shaft is all the more beautiful for its narrow range. It is still in the minority, as it were, against the overwhelming mass of the storm clouds. Yet the penetration of the cloud bank by the spear of radiance from the concealed heavenly upper world is a promise of greater revelation, further enlightenment to come. It means the clouds are beginning to part and that, sooner or later, there will be a full sunny sky. All we need to do is wait, and it is easier to do that having seen the initial glimpse. The first shaft of light means that more, much more, is on its way.

But, as in "Chain Lightning" (*Presto*, 1989), here we have more than just a cameo preservation of a moment of Nature's beauty. Rather, lyricist Peart sees the moment as a parable for a key insight about life. It is not just the fairly trivial hope for a nice, sunny sky that he is writing about, but rather the energizing vision of possibility for all things, for a fulfilling life.

Before we can penetrate any further into the song, we must get straight precisely what the strange-sounding, apparently ill-fitting title has to do with anything. After all, there seems nary a ladder to be found in the song's words. But there is. Indeed there is. In fact, what we have here is one more of the many biblical images in Rush's songs, something all the more remarkable in view of the group's apparent antipathy towards conventional religion. At any rate, this time the reference is to the story of the encounter of the patriarch Jacob with God at the site of what later became the city of Bethel. Here it is, slightly condensed, from Genesis 28.

> Jacob came to a certain place and stayed there that night because the sun had set. Taking one of the stones of the place, he put it under his head and lay down to sleep. And he dreamed that there was a ladder set up on the earth, and the top of it reached to heaven; and behold, the angels of God were climbing up and down on it. And behold, the Lord stood upon it and said, "I am Jehovah, the God of your fathers. The land on which you lie I will give to you and to your descendants. Behold, I am with you and will keep watch over you wherever you go." And Jacob awoke from his sleep and said, "How awesome is this place! This is none other than the house of God, and this is the gate of heaven!"

Now, what's the point? Well, isn't the shaft of advancing light that breaks through the rain clouds something of a ladder from heaven to earth? Not in the strictly religious sense, of course; in the Bible, the point of the story, with its ancient, childlike thought forms, is that Jacob had actually stumbled upon God's front door, the place where the spheres meet. Presumably, Jacob himself could have climbed the pearly rungs and snuck into heaven, à la Jack and the Bean Stalk. But the symbolism is clear: the shaft of refugee sunlight marks a path whereby the ever-eager mind of a human being may ascend to loftier heights of possibility, broader ranges of vision, wider perspectives on life and self. This Jacob's ladder is not exactly a vision into the future, since the future does not yet exist to be seen (despite the fraudulant claims of the superstition mongers lampooned in "Free Will"); instead, it provides a glimpse of what the future, your future in particular, *could* be.

What Peart describes in this song is something like a moment of *satori*, or sudden enlightenment, in Zen Buddhism. The truth may dawn suddenly, provoked by the simplest of happenstances. One is caught off guard, and suddenly some insight, perceived despite oneself when the barriers of jaded expectation are down, transforms one. For instance, it was an abrupt slap in the face from a cantankerous old Zen master that jolted one seeker over the threshold of enlightenment, according to a famous Zen anecdote. It was some insignificant event that caused philosopher-mystic Friedrich Nietzsche on the way home from the library to be struck one ordinary afternoon with the insight that all things return eternally, to happen over and over again forever.

With us, it may not be anything so exotic, anything so esoteric. But a vision of hope, of possibility where you had thought there was none, is a real revelation not to be despised. What will trigger it? Perhaps a smile on a face that is usually turned toward you with a frown. Perhaps a swirl of leaves about your feet on an autumn afternoon. Perhaps some treasured words from a loved one long estranged. Perhaps the sight of a stray shaft of light after a rain shower. Or perhaps a song about one.

"The Pass"

For the next song, let us descend from visionary heights down to the depths of despair. "The Pass" (*Presto*, 1989) deals with the current epidemic of teenage suicide, tragic but also ironic, since here we are seeing people despair of life's possibilities at an age when they have scarcely had a chance to see what those possibilities are. Lack of hope is the problem, or maybe it is too narrow a view of the chances, the lack of a dream, or the lack of fuel to keep the dream going.

The scene opens on a high school youth clad, no doubt, in the traditional leather jacket as befits the role he desperately wants to play. He proudly swaggers out of the schoolyard expecting his peers' applause for his reprise of the role first played well by Marlon Brando many years ago, as the archetypal macho, hard-as-nails tough guy, a schoolyard stoic sporting a greased back DA haircut.

But the applause won't come, perhaps because there are too many auditioning for the role for anyone to notice him. Or if it comes, it is hollow, maybe because the lone figure is too sensitive, too intelligent for his own good. And the approval of his peers seems hollow, futile, disappointing. At any rate, his swagger, as all swaggers do, serves merely to conceal a cancerous growth of despair, of self-doubt, of doubt that life is worth living. The glories of peer-group acceptance, solidarity around superficial values, is too insubstantial, a fleeting wraith, a game too easy to win and therefore hardly worth winning. Is there nothing more?

The surface persona of a rebel with no conscience fades imperceptibly into that of a martyr with no cause. Our would-be hero is about to cash it all in. He has won the game, all right, the only game he knows, but—by default. And so now he considers a martyr's death.

But a martyr, by definition, yields up his life in witness to some cause that he would sooner die for than betray. Yet the song's protagonist ponders dying in witness to the sad fact there is no available cause worth either dying or *living* for.

All too dimly does this sensitive soul trapped in a stifling social matrix of limited horizons perceive that there is something else, something far better to live for, but he is (once again) like the poor denizens of Plato's Twilight Cave. He can but discern shadows of vaster things. There is static on his frequency, clouding perceptions of what he desperately needs to see. There is a lightning storm in his veins, a turbulence of frustration for raging at unattainable glory, straining at intangible bonds. What stops him from seeing, from knowing the glory that would make life more than an empty shadow play?

That's what's brought our nihilistic hero to the vertigo-brink of premature suicide. He finds himself trembling on a rocky verge, staring down into the maelstrom. He can no longer face life on the razor's edge. Nothing's turned out as he thought it would. What is this razor's edge? It is the thin border between hope and despair, an easy one to fall off, like the Chinvat Bridge of Zoroastrian mythology, the sword blade bridge on which every soul one day stands, ready to be propelled off into the yawning gulf of Hell by the fatal weight of a single sin.

Even so, everything may appear to be going along just fine, with every goal attained, until a momentary flash of unwelcome insight makes you inescapably aware that all was for naught, all pointless. The emptiness of things is revealed, and there opens the Pit at your very feet. There begins to sound in your ears the whisper of suicide. It happens in a moment, which is why we are so often astonished at a suicide. "She had everything going for her! Not a care in the world that I knew about! Why?"

But that whisper is hardly the voice you need to hear at such a moment. No, what you need to hear is that of another like yourself who perhaps has endured the same hell of momentary despair, yet withdrawn from the craggy edge of self-destruction. Isolation from others speeds one down the path to suicide. Do we have no friends, or at least none we can be open with, without fear of rejection? If we do have them, the danger will never be so great, because a friend's words, his advice, even his listening heart will act as a kind of mirror enabling us to see that things may not seem so black, that there are indeed those stray sparks of hope's candlelight burning to guide us. You are hearing such a voice in this song: everyone gets lost in the dark at one time or another, but one is more likely to get lost alone than with companions. Misery does in fact love company; the cliché is true! Because company lessens the misery. Why not?

Why does suicide seem not only a way out of our problems, but actually a heroic way? If you think about it, it should seem rather cowardly, since suicide is just seeking the escape hatch instead of trying harder to deal with one's problems. But we do not see this because of a false mystique that has grown up about suicide. Somewhere we have gotten the idea that suicide has something romantic, even heroic, about it, the act of a noble warrior—but in fact it is the failure of nerve on the part of one who in the end simply loses the will to fight. And if you follow in that coward's footsteps, you'll be no tragic hero; there will be no valor to praise, no cheering throngs to light your funeral pyre of glory.

What is the answer to despair? Certainly not the absolute avoidance of tragedy, total success in steering clear of pitfalls. No one can do that, this world being what it is, people being what they are. Again, sooner or later, everyone gets lost in the dark. Why then do we not all seek the suicide's way out? Granted, it may be that the darkness of some of us is not so deep, but then again our problems, objectively considered, may not really be so great as we think, and the darkness still looks Stygian to us!

No, the difference is the dream. Even though they may be plunged in velvet darkness, those who want to be captains of their fate learn to steer by the stars. Like the ship's navigator, we all find it easier steering in noonday's floodlight, but we needn't stand still or drift when night comes, because if we know where to look, there will always be points of light scattered here and there throughout the blackness of the night sky. You just have to know those sparks of hope well enough to chart your course by them. And that takes preoccupation with the possible, fixation on hope. It means cultivating your dreams. It means learning that despair isn't the result of failing (this time) to attain your dreams; rather, despair comes when you let the embers of your dreams go out. And that is precisely what the suicide is doing. In fact, he is extinguishing them, blowing them out like candles on a deathday cake.

Sooner or later, all of us do our time in the gutter. But the thing about dreamers is that they look at the cars zooming by them and start planning on what kind they want to drive when they get back behind the wheel, as they are sure they will. In fact, though we will discuss the song in another chapter, it may not be out of place to bring in a reference here to "Red Barchetta," since in some ways that song also uses driving a car as a symbol of motivation and of the daring dash of life lived under your own initiative and direction. But no one finds himself behind the wheel all the time. Sometimes you are at the side of the road, even in the gutter (if not actually "Beneath the Wheels"!), sitting back with no options at the moment except to assess where you are, how you got there, and where you want to go next. And how you can get ahold of another Barchetta, red or otherwise. But it's not the time

CAROL SELBY PRICE

to despair. This road may be barricaded, true, but maybe there are other ways out of town.

Really, what we're talking about here is *endurance*, and the next two songs deal in some detail with this factor, so to them we now turn.

"Vital Signs"

If the opposite of dreams in "The Pass" was deadly despair, hope's opposite in "Vital Signs" (*Moving Pictures*, 1981) is deadening conformity. Here we find some of the same themes we considered in an earlier chapter ("The Mass Production Zone," Chapter II). This song speaks eloquently and evocatively of the ferment of youth, the time when one decides what one is to be and what life is to mean. In this period everyone witnesses and experiences the truth articulated by the Existentialist philosopher, novelist, and playwright Jean Paul Sartre, that with human beings, "existence precedes essence." That is, we are unlike animals whose nature is entirely defined for them by heredity and environment. Though we, too, are to a great degree defined by these factors, there is one great difference. We have *freedom*.

There are many more options open to us in the environment which not only nature but men and women before us have created. With us, the shape of our bodies, the number of our senses, and other such biological "givens" are not the half of it. True, these features in some measure serve to draw the parameters of the game board of life, but much is left to us. There is no true "human nature" as such, that would accurately describe all human beings. No, each is an individual and can "authenticate" his or her own existence through the actions one chooses to perform. You might say that "you are what you do," not what you have inherited from chromosomes and genes.

In the period of youth, then, it is given us to scan the menu of possibilities and to decide what would be right for us. Especially in our culture, this is no easy process. Since there are so many options for careers, even for identities (a good thing in itself), many find themselves paralyzed before the bewildering range of alternatives, stricken by the shock of "overchoice."

Picture once more Dustin Hoffman's character in *The Graduate*: he stands passively at his own graduation party, a silent sounding board for all the unwanted advice of adults, each with his own set of self-imposed blinders, each with his own agenda to push. Each and all tell him what he would be wise to do with his life. Eventually he rejects all these attempted manipulations, but that is only half the Graduate's problem. The real difficulty is that he stands motionless before the great galaxy of possibilities without a clue as to how to decide which to choose. He is just like the donkey in the fable who starved to death while standing in front of two tasty-looking haystacks—because

108

he couldn't decide which to start munching first! It was always so much simpler for young people in less advanced societies, or those in which choices were restricted according to one's caste or race. But who wants such simplicity? Better the risk of making the wrong choice, especially since one can usually start over. Not every choice is a final one, or irrevocable.

The opening words of "Vital Signs" describe this period of exciting uncertainty quite well. It is an unstable condition, but that's only what we should expect. The only things that are stable are petrified stone, cold metal. But instability is a condition of life, a prerequisite for mental or environmental change. There are both the changes within us (mental) and without us (environmental) to cope with, as well as the question as to which affects which! Is your environment changing because your mental changes give you a new perspective on it? Or do your new perspectives and insights actually lead you to change your environment, as did the student radicals of the Sixties?

You start to know new people, and old people in new ways. New beliefs split old friendships and cement new ones. New freedoms alienate you from your parents—or perhaps enable you to see things as your parents do for the first time! Sparks will fly! You are confused but excited by the crackle of atmospheric disturbance, the fever of flux, drunk on the wild wine of human interface and interchange.

This period of new freedom and new responsibility, of genuine self-creation, is a traumatic one. Since the ground is shaky and the path before one uncertain, one's destination largely unknown—how easy to take a false step! More than one! How many people we alienate! What fools we make of ourselves—not that it can really be helped! It's all part of the process, and everyone has his past embarrassments to rue. We do our best, but we are groping. Our impulse is pure, but sometimes it short-circuits due to *external* interference. Think of the Graduate's mob of unwanted advisors. Think, too, of all the stupid advice television gives you, since TV is really just propaganda for the junk-merchants who victimize impressionable youth like vampires sucking a juicy neck!

And for young people, so sensitive to the pressure from their peers, perhaps the worst kind of external interference is that from the Crowd (better, the Herd). In youth we gain a picture of who we are to a great degree by how others see us. In early youth, we care most about how parents and teachers see us. A bit later, the others whose approval we seek are those we run with: our friends or those we desperately *wish* were our friends. So we may try very hard to conform to the standards of the pack. How else can you account for the fact, already noticed in an earlier chapter, that many young people carry fashions and dress styles to the extent of virtually wearing team uniforms!? (In the case of urban youth gangs, the final step has been taken: their jackets have actually become literal uniforms, and, as in "Territories," they *will* shoot you just for the color of your shirt!)

Right here we see the great alternative to dreams in "Vital Signs"—*conformity.* To put it simply, the expectations of the crowd, even a crowd that you like, a crowd of well-intended friends, work like a kind of gravity to prevent your life from blasting off into its own unique future. Dreams are the fuel for the rocket, and if one is to attain escape velocity, the fuel of dreams must be stronger than the gravity of the crowd's expectations.

It can't really be any other way, can it? Your own potential is a highly individual thing, suited uniquely to you, made possible by your unique combination of talents and desires. This is no less true for every member of every crowd, but for some reason the crowd seeks to stifle all individual destinies, to obscure all individual paths. When you strive to live up to the in-crowd's expectations, you cannot see the way for *you.* An ounce of perception is worth a pound of obscure.

Why does the crowd smother individual uniqueness? Wouldn't it be in everyone's best interest to pursue his or her own path instead of all trying to fit in the same niche, all trying to be the same stereotyped person? Sure it would, but the problem is that to follow your own path instead of being a Madonna "Wanna-Be" is that no one likes to go it alone. There is safety in numbers, or so it seems as we huddle like cavemen around the campfire of mediocrity, in deadly fear of what might be out there awaiting us. What if it were excitement? What if it were fulfillment? But we will never know as long as we cling pathetically to the safety of the "norm." What we don't know won't hurt us, but then again, we won't know what we're missing either!

It is to the creative and courageous transcendence of the mediocre norm that Rush calls us in "Vital Signs." Everyone owes it to himself to deviate from the norm, to elevate from it, or in other words, to transcend the conventional norm of mediocrity.

Seen another way, we are talking about what Carl Jung called the process of "individuation." It is easy enough, indeed inevitable, to have an Ego, a self understood as the natural product of heredity, environment, upbringing, and social influence. But that's really just the egg, just the cocoon. Our business in life is to blossom forth into our unique personhood, the Self. (That hardly implies selfishness; indeed, the resultant Self will probably be more self-giving and concerned for others, not less.) To do this, we must develop away from the "norm," as Rush calls it, for this is after all the lowest common denominator.

One of many possible examples we could draw from the world of youth movies would be what happens to Tony Manero in the hilarious 1979 satire of the Disco craze, *Saturday Night Fever.* At the beginning of the film, Tony is riding high. He is the king of the local disco, respected, loved, and lusted after by everybody he knows. He is the swaggering epitome of Cool. He succeeds so well precisely because he is the incarnation of "the norm." He embodies it; he personifies it. Everybody else in his loser neighborhood wants to be like him insofar as they want to conform to the cool Disco stereotype. Things are cruising along just fine until one day a series of events begin that start awakening the poor jerk to just what a fool he's been. He begins to realize that to embrace the lowest common denominator, and to do it well, is to *excel in mediocrity*, to live in two dimensions only. By the end of the film, his dreams have awakened, just a bit. He sees a glimpse of a broader vista and decides to leave his loser buddies and dead-end, hedonistic lifestyle behind.

On a completely different level, one could look at Hermann Hesse's spiritual classic *Siddhartha*. Here is a novel about a young man in India in the days of Gotama Buddha. He passes through several stages of a personal quest for identity and enlightenment, largely paralleling the personal odyssey of the Buddha himself. Siddhartha tries out the harsh life of monasticism, the wildfires of hedonistic abandon, the settled existence of family life with its heartbreaks. At one point he actually considers becoming a disciple of the Buddha, whom he meets, but at the last he turns aside to continue his quest in his own direction.

The Buddha's own spiritual biography shows that he, too, was an innovator, a rejector of norms, a spurner of well-trodden paths. And Hesse's point seems to be that if one is to follow such a spiritual master in truth, the last thing to do is to take the same path he himself trod! Did the Buddha follow anyone else's path? No! Well, if you are to take any inspiration from him, neither must you follow *his* path! You must strike out on your own, even as he did. You cannot follow the example of a trailblazer by walking a well-marked path—even if it is the trail he blazed!

The real individualist does not create a new norm; rather he urges others to decide for themselves what *their* norm shall be. How often great thinkers have gone unheard by their closest followers! Why are the most eager to hear also often the deafest? Recall the scene in *Monty Python's Life of Brian* in which reluctant messiah Brian of Nazareth, drafted as a savior by his fans, urges the crowd, "You've got to think for *yourselves!*," to which they adoringly reply with one voice, "Yes! We've got to think for ourselves!"

Conformity is comfortable; conformity is easy. Individuation is difficult. You have to try to make sense of all the conflicting signals, to piece together the truth from the chaos you're picking up. This takes patience. Picture yourself, let's say, an android escaping from the Mass-Production Zone, trying to survive by altering your own programming. You've got to pause, rewind, replay. A dormant memory chip begins to warm up. Here comes the flood of memories from when you used to be a human being: you sample them at random—there! Hold the one you need.

Once you discern the path that is yours, you discover how difficult it will be to tread it alone. Not to say that individuality excludes having friends, but your real friends will understand that you must follow your own light, and they will be your companions in that they, too, are pursuing their own dreams. Pursuing your own destiny is like climbing a mountain: it can't be done *for* you, and it is going to take endurance. Endurance, in turn, depends on the strength of your dream. Do you really believe in it? Is it really worth what you will have to sacrifice? Without that faith, why bother? *With* that faith, you're already half way there. Forget the daydreams of fiction. The sober fact is that the friction from obstacles in your path will only be worn smooth by persistence.

You must determine, as the Buddha and Hesse's Siddhartha did, that nothing will stand in your way, that there are no conditions, *e.g.*, "I will strive to attain my goal so long as no one opposes me, as long as public opinion is in my favor, providing I can do it while getting rich, etc." Sorry, that kind of double-mindedness will never make it. Do you want it or not? Drop all the conditions. Unconditional courage and conviction alone can drag this dream across the finish line.

"Marathon"

"Marathon" (*Power Windows*, 1985) carries the same themes further, only this time the focus is not on the alternatives to dreams, but rather on the difficult process of sticking to your dreams over the long haul. As the title implies, this song compares life to a long-distance run. Life is a marathon, not a sprint. At least it should be. The song rejects the "live fast; die early" model of life so inexplicably popular in some quarters. If life were intended as a sprint, fine; a short life, shooting your wad as fast as you can, would be the way to do it. But it is not. The truth is rather that life is a long-distance run, and if you end it fast, it's only because you paced yourself poorly and dropped out somewhere along the way.

It's a steady pace that will get you there, not a frantic burst of speed that you can't maintain. It's not so much a matter of your speed as it is the force that goes into the flow. If you hit a steady pace you can let the race take care of itself. Here's an important insight: a great deal of the pressure's off once you realize that you needn't do everything, accomplish everything, learn all the answers, in the next year, or the next five or ten years. That's what you've got a whole life for! Survival till tomorrow is just the minimum goal. Life, after all, is a journey, and you want to be able to see some of the sights along the way! It's more than just a dash for survival, not just a flash in the pan. The race is in the running itself, not just in the dotted line you cross at the end of it! So calm down; try for a steady pace. That way you'll go the distance.

To put it another way, it would be easier if life's goals could be met suddenly with a great burst of speed, but they can't. And therefore you can't get it all out of the way in advance and then settle back to enjoy it. The reason for this is that life's goals aren't just a series of tasks to accomplish, like Hercules's twelve labors. Life's aims aren't just a wish list of goodies you'd like to round up sooner or later and hopefully sooner. (It's more than blind ambition, than simple greed.) No, though there may indeed be many such tasks, many such goals, all legitimate, the key insight is that the marathon race of life is a necessarily slow and gradual process of passing various milestones *within*.

There is a process of maturation you have to go through, and you can't hurry it up much. You have to go through the paces. You have to experience a large number of people, conditions, challenges, before your character crystallizes. It is a chemical process of sorts. You can't speed up the reaction time. Just keep going and let it happen, because happen it will. That is, unless you start cheating, taking shortcuts, bypassing necessary experiences, trying to grow up too fast.

It could be argued that we are seeing a great deal of such shortcutting in our society, where thanks to the cynical greed of advertisers, kids are being pushed into sexual maturity and a false social maturity where cool cynicism passes for sophistication. One day soon we're liable to see Rodney Dangerfield's joke become a fulfilled prophecy: birth control pills shaped like Fred Flintstone! What a paradox! Children who are jaded before they ever mature—and they probably *won't* mature, at least not emotionally, as a result! Thanks, Calvin Klein! Thanks, MTV!

You might think a sprint is a harder race to run than a marathon because it takes such a concentrated burst of energy. But any runner will tell you that it is much more of a challenge to keep feeding out that energy at a controlled clip over a long distance. And like it or not, that is just what life requires of us. Or, to be more precise, that is the requirement of a life lived with a dream, with aspirations that you yourself have chosen and that mean something to you.

Without dreams, the race metaphor may be completely inappropriate. This is because a race has a *goal*. Not just a dotted line, that's true, but all that means is that life is a race with an *interior* goal, not an exterior one. You're not living if you're pursuing a goal someone else set. That is what the Existentialist Heidegger called "inauthentic existence." And if you are just living your life from day to day with no goal at all, you are certainly not running a race. You are just taking a stroll. There is no question of pace, or even of direction.

Pursuing a dream of your own, then, is what takes the endurance. The test of ultimate will for every serious runner is that heartbreak climb uphill. He must pick up the pace if he wants to stay in the race. Why "heartbreak?" Of course, it's a well-known runner's term. Sooner or later in every race comes "heartbreak hill," the turning

113

point where your second wind had better make its appearance. But there may be all sorts of heartbreaks awaiting you in life's race, and they, too, will take some emotional adrenalin.

Well, what must you endure? At the worst, you may have to endure active opposition from those who dismiss your vision as Quixotic, fantastic. In college those who decide to major in philosophy often are greeted with shocked stares of disbelief from friends and parents. "How can you ever make a living at *that?!*" Those who set their sights on the performing arts may hear similar cries of outrage: "But do you realize how many people there are in those fields already unable to make a living at it!?" Naturally, there's no point in being stubborn, in refusing to listen to rational arguments from people with experience. It would, admittedly, be useful to know the prospects. And there might indeed be little point in deciding to make your living as a wandering juggler.

But if it's a question of whether you're going to do what you feel called to do versus just making money at a soul-killing drone job, we *are* talking about enduring opposition for the sake of your dreams. Don't sell them out!

But it need not be overt opposition. The passage of *time itself* must be endured if your dream-goal is one that requires a good length of time for its realization. The more it means to you, the more the simple endurance of months and years without its precious realization is felt as a burden not easily borne. It seems that time itself is opposition. It seems as if you are swimming against the stream of inertia, making the heartbreak climb up the hill.

What makes the long climb possible is that the very cherishing of the hope is sweet, a foretaste of the thing itself. Indeed, how often do we find that anticipation is the sweetest taste of all?!

There *are* momentary, fragmentary realizations, and they, too, keep us going. The beginning musician may feel pretty mediocre, like she's going nowhere, until one day she hits a longer than usual series of the right notes in sequence! Even though she may not be able to do it again that day or that week, she keeps going with renewed vigor because now she is assured that somewhere within her is the ability, and that one day it will blossom forth in full.

We experience more and more such moments as we run unflaggingly along, and they make it much easier to make it to and *past* the next milestone. But none is an end in itself. We can't stop till we attain it, or we will betray the dream. Indeed, that may mean we *never* stop! There will always be room for improvement, for finer honing of our skills, even if we ourselves are the only remaining competition! From the starting gun to the finish line, the peak is never passed. The true prospect of glory must be an ever-receding will-o'-the-wisp that keeps you running in pursuit. Since the race itself, not the finish line, is the real goal, then to stop running is by definition to lose, even if you come in first. To win is precisely never to give up the race!

One thing, though: endurance isn't workaholism; it's not fanaticism. If you don't take the occasional rest break, you might as well be trying to cover the whole marathon track at a sprinter's pace. You'll burn yourself out either way. So that your meters don't overload, why not stop for a few moments' rest by the side of the road? (Perhaps this is what you are really doing when you think you are stuck doing time in the gutter!) You can afford to miss a stride.

But you'd best remember to get back up! You don't have to worry about catching up with and passing everybody else. Really, you're not racing against them anyway. You're pacing against inertia. This marathon of life is really more like a road trip than a road race, if you think about it. Haven't you ever been on the highway for a long trip somewhere and sooner or later noticed that you start to pass, and to be passed by, the same cars over and over again? There's a momentary feeling of futility; you start to think, "Gee, I can't seem to make any progress against this guy!" But then sanity prevails: "What am I *talking* about? I'm not racing this guy! I'm taking my own route at my own clip to my own goal! Who *cares* where this car is in relation to me?" So with the marathon of life.

As long as you realize that it's going to take your endurance, that no one gets a free ride, that success will be more than a lucky shot in the dark, you'll be okay.

Why do we drop out? Or why are we tempted to, anyway? Discouragement, isn't it? Every time we look up at our goal, it still seems so far off, and we groan, "What's the point? I'll never make it!" But this is a fatal confusion. Of course you're not there yet! This is a marathon, not a sprint, after all! The proper thing to get discouraged about is not being where you *could* be in your progress *at this particular point in time*! And even so, what's the big deal? Just get up and get going! Was your dream expecting you at a particular minute?

"Mission"

In general we would have to say that Rush's vision of dreams and endurance is quite democratic, that it most often seems in Peart's lyrics that any listener is being assured that he or she can carry the aspiration all the way to the finish line, that any suggestion to the contrary is just more promediocrity, proconformism propaganda issued by the lords of the Mass Production Zone. Yet in "Mission" (*Hold Your Fire*, 1987), we seem to catch a new and strange note. What a cynic might call a harsh note of reality seems to have intruded.

Suddenly it sounds as if Peart thinks that there are only certain gifted individuals who have any hope of achieving the desired greatness. They are, perhaps, identical with Colin Wilson's "Five Percent," those whose possession of "Faculty X" makes them, for better or for worse, "Outsiders." Before we go on to examine what "Mission" has to say about the pride as well as the plight of these creative geniuses, we really ought to give another moment's attention to this ticklish question of whether Rush's democratic vision of hope has vanished.

Keeping in mind, first, that Rush has acknowledged as a major inspiration the philosophy of Ayn Rand, we ought to be a bit surprised at any apparent implication in their lyrics that all people are created equal. Now maybe they should all be *treated* equally, that is, given equal opportunity; that's perfectly realistic: unequally gifted people will then rise or sink to their proper level, according to ability or effort. There is a uniquely modern fetish for equality, however, that causes some social planners to close their eyes (hidden behind rose-colored glasses in the first place), and simply pretend that all are in fact equal, whether they are or not.

Well, this is quite another thing, the very sort of nonsense Rand attacked with a vengeance. It is just this sort of policy that forbids the excellent to excel, lest the inferiority of the inferior be revealed. For inferiority, inequality of ability, simply will not go away; if we are not to see it, it must be hidden, or we must become blind to it.

Rand and Rush, on the other hand, want to see. And clearly. If the blind belief in automatic equality prevails, then not even the excellent will any longer bother to excel, since they will not be allowed to, nor be rewarded for it. They will not even see the need to excel, nor feel guilty for not excelling. Everyone will have only mediocre sites to aim for.

So to hold forth an elite standard is just what we would have expected from Rush. The surprise is that we usually hear an apparent blanket assurance to listeners one-and-all that "Come on! You can do it!"

Here's the solution. Rush's music is not aimed scatter-gun at any and all possible listeners, but only at their actual listeners. These make up a pretty steady and closely defined clientele, almost a club with a self-selected membership. Listeners who don't sense in themselves the spark of ability aren't going to be attracted by lyrics like this. One suspects that the Rush listenership is thickly populated with Outsiders. It is to these people that Rush speaks its message of aspiration and endurance.

"Mission" is a meditation on the drives and demons of the greatly gifted. The real genius is the one born both with great ability, and with an inborn drive that will allow him to see that ability. The great creator has little choice in the matter: he must create or be himself destroyed! Such is the power of the creative urges swelling within! Such is the innate life, the almost independent existence, of the ideas, designs, and concepts that seem to spring full-blown to the minds of the true artists!

And pity the artistic genius who is not up to bearing the burden his greatness forces upon him! There is no guarantee that Nature has endowed you with the psychic resiliency or stamina you need to roll with the punches your Muse will deliver to you!

Ancient Arabian poets told how their calling as poets came upon them suddenly and without warning. They might be walking peacefully through the marketplace, nodding to friends as they pass, minding their own business, when suddenly a *jinni* would strike! The inspiring poetic genius had picked out the poor unfortunate, like it or not! The inflicting spirit would drive the poet-to-be to his knees and begin to choke him, with bystanders all aghast, until with his first sputterings he began to haltingly croak out rhyming oracular couplets! Henceforward, despite himself, he was a poet—or a madman, for the Arabic term *kahin* meant both. For the Greek poet (or artist or musician or dramatist or prophet) to be inspired by the Muse was pretty much the same proposition, to be in the grip of a nameless possession.

We now use some of these words ("inspiration," "the Muse") in a purely figurative sense, but isn't the ancient conception in some ways pretty close to the observed facts? Think of how many of the great artists of all kinds have been tormented souls. A recent medical survey shows that over eighty percent of all writers have some type of depressive affliction, bipolar ("manic-depressive") or monopolar (just "manic" with no "off" switch!). Many are borderline schizoid. This can hardly be coincidence! It is the same setting of the brain mechanism that both opens up the channel to the subconscious (or the creative "Left Brain"—see Chapter VII) and creates psychic static on the line. By the same token, many of the great writers and artists seem to have no social, romantic, or real-world competency. Their spirits fly on dangerous missions, their imaginations on fire. Focused high on soaring ambitions, they may seem to be of no earthly use in the eyes of the pragmatic. They can't help it: all their energy is consumed in a single desire. It is as if all their energy is focused, to the anguish and chagrin of their friends and families, on the creative task. None is left for mundane life. It is not a conscious choice they make; rather their Muse seems to have made it for them. No doubt van Gogh with the madly blazing canvasses, his feverish pictures, and the severed ear is the great prototype here.

What a cost must be borne by the true and great genius! He pays a fearful price for his glimpse of paradise. His service to the unmerciful Muse is a hard and, in the last analysis, an involuntary one. He is a slave driven by his obsession. The mania of the Muse is chief among the secrets that set the genius apart from the run of the mill. How many have prayed for blessed release from the curse that the rest of us, seeing the fruit of their labors, must consider a blessing! "To hell with inspiration! Just give me peace of mind!" Such was the last

117

temptation of Christ, as Nikos Kazantzakis, an artist and visionary him-self, knew only too well.

To the rest of us, the lives of the geniuses are as much objects of awe as their works themselves! Perhaps we would not even suspect greatness to be possible had we not seen the wonders produced through their guided hands. What thoughts, what dreams are coming to birth as the engaged eye sweeps across the vista of past genius? As they gaze on the monuments of artistic genius in the ages past, new generations of the Muse-inspired enlist for their arduous tasks. Thus are recruited the ever-new ranks of composers, musicians, poets, novelists, painters, di-rectors, architects.

As they pause to gaze longer than the rest of us, who may sim-ply view exposure to these great works as a boring trip to the museum, these sensitive souls hear a silent whisper of "Follow me..." echoing through the halls of the Artists' Valhalla. And what words are silently echoing through the spirits of those lost in admiration? We wish we had their instinct, their drive...and their dreams.

The song proceeds to advise those listeners who can identify with such an experience, and no doubt some of them have had such thoughts and aspirations awakened by listening to Rush. They must re-solve to hold their fire, keep it burning bright until the dream ignites. In the Gospel of Thomas Jesus says, "I have cast a fire upon the world, and behold, I guard it until it is ablaze" (Saying 10). This is the spark of awakening aspiration, before results are there to keep the artist en-couraged. It is a period of preparation, of writing practice novels you know will never sell, of composing songs that sound a bit too much like those that inspired you.

During this time the great challenge is to maintain your dedi-cation, your momentum. You must reawaken it continually, reassure yourself of the spark of talent you see, even if no one else can spot it yet. You must hold your fire, not in the sense of the cliché, that of not shooting your gun, but rather hold onto your fire, your internal fire, the fire of your dream. Tend it! Don't let it go out! Dreams needn't be always in motion for their spark to stay alive.

But this advice is dangerous! In fact the depiction of the tor-mented, obsessed artist throughout the whole song has been intended as a warning! Are you really sure you want artistic success if this is the price? This may be the last choice you will have in the matter! Once the Muse, that spirit with a vision, that dream with a mission, gets hold of you, it will be full speed ahead. You will have to obey that artistic compulsion, like it or not.

There is a crucial difference between the preliminary stage of dream and the subsequent stage of obsession. If you tend the fire long enough, at length feeding it with the potent fuel of action, the resultant pride in your work and its reception will make the crucial difference, and there will be no going back! Artistic creation becomes an addiction. Obsession has to have action, and always more. It is a hard and narrow road, and few there are who find it.

What of the many who do not? Actually, to some who are relieved at not having to undergo the trials of the great artists, it may rather be a comforting rationalization. A good excuse to take the easier path, when deep down you know you could have and perhaps should have taken the harder one. But the one who just hasn't got what it takes in either talent or dedication is scarcely comforted. Unless, of course, they can somehow take some comfort in the next song, of which they are the theme.

"Middletown Dreams"

Dreams come in for a rather different treatment in "Middletown Dreams" (*Power Windows*, 1985) than we have seen before. The title itself may warn us that we are in for something different. "Middletown" means Anywhere USA, any and everywhere, the typical scene. Though Rush's songs, as we have just seen, tend to function as pep talks aimed at the gifted, urging them to pursue their dreams and aspirations, to arrive atop the Olympus of the great, it is clear that not everyone has the requisite ability. What role can dreams play for them? That is the subject of this song.

In short, dreams function for the rest of us pretty much as Karl Marx said religion functions for the oppressed masses, as an "opiate of the people." Marx's words on this subject are often misconstrued. Despite the fanatical persecution of religion by the Communist authorities who considered themselves Marx's ideological heirs, Marx did not mean to paint religious faith as a drug which keeps people in a deluded stupor, unable to see the truth about the world and themselves. Rather, he seems to have meant that religion served as a comfort in a wretched world, although it was nothing more than a band-aid solution where radical surgery was really required.

Rush seems to be saying that there are some people (sadly, perhaps most people) whose dreams do not function as rocket fuel to an exciting and dynamic future, but in the absence of such a future their dreams can at least make it possible for them to drown their sorrows. Dreams can provide a cushion against a too-harsh reality. In his book, *The Feast of Fools*, Harvey Cox speaks of the need for fantasy to provide a "horizon" in one's life, a wide-open sky instead of a depressingly low ceiling imposed by cruel mundane reality. Otherwise, the daily, unspectacular routine becomes a soul-killing grind. The great modern fantasy author J. R. R. Tolkien once answered an objector who disapproved of fantastic literature on the ground that it supposedly took people's mind off the pressing questions of the day. He asked in reply, why should we demand of a prisoner that he think of nothing but his cell? Why indeed!

In our culture people readily seek the wider horizons of a fantasy life by renting videos, watching soap operas, doting over the affairs of celebrities. But this is not what Tolkien, Cox, or Rush is talking about. What is the difference? Simply that these great American pastimes tend to furnish us with only vicarious experience. The celebrity magazines (whether *People* or *Metal*) are inviting us to despise and reject our own miserable, loathsome, insignificant lives, and to temporarily pretend we are living someone else's.

By contrast, the sort of dreams fostered by Rush's songs, Cox's visions, and Tolkien's epic fiction encourage us to imagine our own lives, our own selves, not as they are, *but as they would be* if they lived on a higher plane, in a higher key. We are still not talking about aspiration, as in some of the previous dream songs, since the dreams most of us dream could not be realized under any circumstances. Yet there is still a stretching, a growing, that ensues as we dream them.

To take Tolkien as an example again, it is hard not to see the hobbit characters (Bilbo, Frodo, Sam Gamgee) as the counterparts of Tolkien and his readers. Clearly, we are to identify with them, not with the Herculean heroes Boromir and Aragorn, nor with the immortal wizard Gandalf. Instead of towering demigods, the hobbits are portly, quaint, and generally pretty silly—just like most of us. Yet it is they who accompany the epic figures like Gandalf on the quests and adventures. In fact, the hobbits are always central to the action. If great deeds are to be done, a Gandalf has need of a Bilbo.

By this Tolkien means to say that modest little people like us are central to history and to true heroism. We may seem anything but heroic, but if we seem minor and mundane to ourselves it is only because we do not see that the myths of figures like Boromir and Aragorn are really the long shadows cast by us and our apparently modest efforts. Do we seem insignificant and trivial next to the heroics of the superheroes of fantasy? It is only because we fail to see that these are stories about us after all.

In epic myth and fantasy there is revealed the truth that you need not slay a dragon or rescue a damsel to be heroic. No, there is a quiet dignity concealed in your outwardly unexceptional life, and it is a real glory. The initiation rituals of all the ancient mystery religions (including Christianity) had the initiate (a humble slob like you or me) symbolically pass through the mythic adventure of the divine hero. That's where the hero myths came from in the first place! The hero is the inner you that could be!

Rush's aspiration songs seem to assume that some can indeed come near to real-live dragon slaying (or its equivalents!), and that these are the great artists and achievers of history. But in "Middletown Dreams," the point is perhaps rather to indicate the quiet greatness of a Middletown life if it allows itself to be nourished on dreams it will never outwardly achieve, if it allows itself to cast long shadows. Let's see if the lyrics bear out this interpretation.

The first stanza seems to recall Arthur Miller's great play, *Death of a Salesman*, as it chronicles the fantasies of a tired salesman who would prefer to attribute greater successes to himself than a cold assessment of reality would warrant. In Miller's play, Willie Loman's tragedy is that he comes to confuse fantasy with reality, and his dreams thus beccme a roadblock to greater striving. Instead of lending perspective to his life, showing how it might be better than it is, his dreams have come to substitute for his life and to function as an excuse for not doing better. Self-deceived and deceiving his family, his life becomes tragic when at the end of his career his mediocrity, his failures, are revealed and the illusion is rudely shattered.

In "Middletown Dreams" things are a bit different. An office door closes early. A hidden bottle comes out of the drawer. A salesman turns and closes the blinds. He finds that he moves a little slower these days; his chair, like his pants, fits a bit more snugly: definitely one of Willie Loman's colleagues, in soul as well as occupation. There is a tragic element here; his dreams do not dawn in clear eyes. They look within, and the dreams come out of a bottle. The salesman cherishes a secret vice, but Sinatra's words ring true for him: Four Roses gets him through the night, and you do have to get through the night. But what are this man's dreams?

He fantasizes one day soon hopping a train and leaving it all behind to take up a vagabond life of rootless adventure. He cannot even remember whether maybe he once seriously planned to do it one day. Doesn't matter. He's doing it now, to all intents and purposes. His ticket is the bottle.

Recall George Bailey, hero of the classic movie *It's a Wonderful Life*. He sees his existence as one long incarceration in an insignificant, provincial small town, with nose to the grindstone. All his life he longs to be up and away, traveling, seeing the world, making himself a part of it. At one point, waiting at the train station for the return of his kid brother from college, he muses, "Y'know what the three most exciting sounds in the world are? Anchor chains, plane motors, and train whistles." And he hopes to be hearing much more of these sounds up close. But it is not to be. He never leaves the small town of Bedford Falls.

Such a life as George Bailey dreamed of would offer our Middletown salesman what he lacks now: not creature comforts (he probably has them), but rather that most precious commodity: freedom. That missing ingredient that makes existence into life: excitement, challenge, daring.

Notice that as the lyrics progress, the train car he wishes he had the guts to hop into merges with the image of the dream per se. Dreams flow across the heartland as if on iron tracks and wooden ties.

121

The locomotive engines of dream are stoked on the fires of desperate imagination. Like boxcars rattling their way across country, dreams transport desires. But those boxcars always hold a certain contraband cargo, too, hobos, the American Gypsies. Dreams transport the ones who need to get out of town. The boxcar is the dream, transporting the salesman, if only in his mind (which is the tiredest part of him) out of town, across the plains of the heartland into more exotic regions beyond. Not the classic ship in a bottle, perhaps, but surely a traincar in a bottle.

But as the train chugs away to parts unknown nearer the bottom of the bottle, another dreamer comes into sight. This one is a young man making his way across the plowed fields of the heartland. It is worth noting that he is accompanied by his best friend, one would think his soul-mate, but the two are not on the same wavelength. One is satisfied with those fields, the other is speeding away, in imagination, as fantasy author Lord Dunsany said, "beyond the fields we know." If he had his way, he and his guitar would be climbing aboard a bus aimed for stardom and excitement.

But we get the distinct feeling he's about as likely to board that celestial omnibus of his imagination as the salesman is to get a berth on that boxcar. It's not going to happen. But he may well play at the local high school dance. He may yet have a gig at a neighborhood nightspot, or set a garage shaking with echoes. And if he does any of these things his life will be far better, much more fulfilled, than if he doesn't. Because the key is self-fulfillment. To become a star isn't going to make him an artist. Being known just means you're more conspicuous, and after a while that thrill palls (as witness Rush's song "Limelight," where we hear of walls that must be built against prying fans and nosey media to keep oneself intact).

The self grows when it stretches its abilities and perfects them, and this is no less true even when one's abilities can only stretch so far! When the guitarist strides onto the high school gym stage and sees his face reflected in the overpolished floorboards, he is not simply indulging a stupid fantasy when he fancies himself reliving the opening of a Beatles concert, a Stones or Rush show. These are the long shadows, greater than his own height, that he casts.

And, again, think of George Bailey: his guardian angel Clarence finally gets him to realize that his decades in Bedford Falls have been an adventure after all! He has come to the rescue of people in distress, enriched many lives in quiet ways, and saved his community from the clutches of Old Man Potter, a foe quite as evil as Tolkien's Sauron, albeit less dramatic (and for that very reason all the more insidious!). The boy with the amateur guitar is like George Bailey and Bilbo Baggins: the epic hero writ small. Sometimes the only way to get the right perspective on something is to look through the eyeglass in reverse after all!

For the third example Rush dishes up a paradox, spotlighting a woman whose spirit withers away precisely because in all her life she has never known the spotlight! (A pity she cannot know she is the focus of this song. But then that would be like knowing whether or not God has predestined you to be saved. No fair.) The middle-aged madonna bears a striking resemblance to Eleanor Rigby, who waits, badly rouged with cosmetics, to greet a romantic visitor who will never come. But wait, he did finally come—the Grim Reaper! How long had she been dead before the stink of corruption brought neighbors to check on her, something they had never done in life? Interred by the similarly lonely Father McKenzie, she perished without a friend.

And isn't our middle-aged maiden just a bit reminiscent of Stella Randolph, the lonely woman in Stephen King's *Cycle of the Werewolf*, passing the nights "lying in her narrow virgin's bed," whose despair is so great that she finally welcomes the furious embrace of the werewolf since no other is liable to be offered her? King's story is allegorical: she has been devoured by her own loneliness.

Rush's portrait is of a hopeless old maid who lives alone in an attic room from which she dreams of someday issuing forth all aglitter, like Cinderella garbed in magic finery supplied by a fairy godmother (who, however, doesn't seem to be listening!). In a blaze of glory she will shake the dust of Middletown from her feet to go paint the town, to trip the light fantastic, to make up for lost time with wine, men, and song. Here you can plug in all that we heard about the siren-call of the city in "Subdivisions," only this overaged madonna, still a mousy virgin as her life slips away, is never going anywhere but down to the supermarket for another armload of tabloids. Her dreams are simply never going to come to life. Yet, for all that, they function as an opiate to dull the pain. They are an intravenous supply of hope seeping steadily into a system that would otherwise succumb to despair.

Every person who'd rather be elsewhere nonetheless understands that their options really do not include ever leaving Middletown. Somebody's got to be in the audience next time Rush tours there. Everybody can't be up on stage. No, the trick is staying sane in Middletown, making life livable there, and dreams are the secret. Accordingly, life's not unpleasant in their little neighborhood precisely because they've learned to dream in Middletown. Not a bad thing to learn.

VII.

MACHINE AND MAN

In this century, technology has advanced not arithmetically but geometrically, exponentially. Thus the world has changed much more in the last few decades than in all of previous human history put together. And with change that significant and that rapid, it's no surprise that sociologists would start talking about *Future Shock* (Alvin Toffler's book and term, but now part of the universal jargon). Too much is happening too fast, and society as a whole hasn't had time to regroup, evaluate, and take stock of all the changes. One segment of society runs ahead, pressing new technologies to the limit, heedless of the impact on other segments of society.

Medical technology has begun to make possible certain things we are not quite sure we want to do, such as prenatal genetic tinkering. While it would allow us to head birth defects off at the pass, wouldn't it also be a dangerous flirtation with Hitler-style eugenics? But until we can somehow arrive at a social consensus on the matter (something never easy to get!), are we supposed to tell scientists they cannot continue research in that direction? Wouldn't that also be dangerously Hitler-like? Are we so afraid of knowledge that we will try to suppress it?

Or how about the military? The Pentagon rushes to apply new technologies to further their own ends, again before the rest of us have a chance to say whether or not we want those ends pursued. Suppose before they'd developed the Atomic Bomb they put it to a vote: "Should we go ahead and finish this thing? Here are the implications. You decide." But there are never votes like this. We are simply presented with the results (sometimes the hard way, as the people of Hiroshima and Nagasaki were!).

Big business (better known to us by now as Big Money) is well known for seizing technology and running away with it, and running over human beings ruthlessly in the process. This is screamingly evident in at least two ways. First, automation constantly makes jobs once done by mere human beings superfluous. Robots can do the same jobs more efficiently and do not demand pay raises! So to hell with flesh-and-blood workers!

Second, production takes precedence over the health of the environment. In a kind of corporate version of the old Epicurean motto, "Let us eat, drink, and be merry, for tomorrow we die!" the corporations decide that they can afford to destroy irreplaceable things like the ozone layer, the tropical rain forests, and any clean air and water supplies—if only they can inch up the profit margin by a few billion more, accumulating money that they themselves could never live long enough to spend! So what if the planet will be out of gas (and everything else!) after the corporate heads have had their little hedonistic joy ride! Their philosophy seems to be that of Louis XIV, "After me, the deluge!"

It is no surprise that the pendulum would eventually swing to the opposite extreme. We are now witnessing a burgeoning anti-science movement that views science as a mistake from the word "go," and regards pollution as the inevitable result of technology. Cancer, say the neo-primitivist gurus, is nature's revenge for science! They seek the comfort of various New Age superstitions, exactly fulfilling the prediction of H. P. Lovecraft in "The Call of Cthulhu" (1926):

> The sciences, each straining in its own direction, have hitherto harmed us little; but some day the piecing together of dissociated knowledge will open up such terrifying vistas of reality, and of our frightful position therein, that we shall either go mad from the revelation or flee from the deadly light into the peace and safety of a new dark age.

In all this turmoil and sludge-slinging polemic, Rush seems to come down as a voice of sanity right in the middle. In the present chapter, we want to examine a few of their songs which deal with technology as both peril and promise, and finally as more than either.

"Red Tide"

Rush has a penchant for songs with the word "Red" in the title. The whole gamut of connotations is exploited, as "red" sometimes stands for rage, or danger, or warning, or even political persuasion. We will deal at greater or lesser length with three of the Red Songs in this chapter, the first (and the most important for our purposes) being "Red Tide" from the 1989 *Presto* album.

As even a casual glance reveals, the song is about impending catastrophe due to pollutants and new, nightmare strains of venereal disease. Let's follow Rush's lyrics as they depict in lurid colors the new team of Apocalyptic Horsemen.

Nature has unleashed some new plague that runs through the streets like an invading horde. Yet new only in detail, different enough from the poxes of the past that the old vaccines do not work. So we re-

125

peat history with a mutant strain. The song's reference seems to be to the Bubonic Plague, or Black Death, which swept through Europe in the fourteenth century, reducing the population by fully one-third, as well as the Red Death of tuberculosis which Poe pictured wreaking similar havoc in the twelfth century. The new contagion will follow in their footsteps, running rampant through the streets. Indeed it is already doing so. We call it AIDS.

Recently, a few isolated cases of Bubonic Plague were discovered in the United States, but there was no genuine plague precisely because we know how to treat it now. We need not worry about history repeating itself to *exactly* the same tune. But we are not ready to deal with something eerily similar that has a new cause and no known cure. AIDS, the new specter, so like the old, is yet definitely a new wrinkle. And therein lies its terrible potency.

Often when we say we are doomed to repeat something, we simply mean to say that it is inevitable; we are seemingly *fated* to repeat it. But here the word "doomed" carries its full force. We are talking about an apocalyptic scenario. AIDS is a plague spread by sex, and people, as if you didn't know, are heedlessly having sex all the time. Africa, already seriously underpopulated, is currently the worst AIDS zone of all. The disease spreads through heterosexual and homosexual channels largely because of rampant prostitution. AIDS activists have a double challenge, because whereas in advanced societies the task is mainly to correct mistaken opinions about how AIDS is spread, in Africa many people just do not believe in AIDS at all! They cannot believe sex could kill them. And even in the most advanced societies, when you are considering a sexual liaison, you are not exactly at your most rational anyway, weighing the alternatives!

When you think about the fact that anyone could possibly have contracted AIDS through a previous sex partner, and that he or she might have it even though a recent blood test says not (since it takes a while for it to show up), any casual sex act becomes a game of Russian roulette! Hence the imagined scene of fugitives at the bedroom door—people fleeing sex like the plague, because it might easily *be* the plague! Or at least having to put passion in neutral while lovers have to pause in their lovemaking to find an open store where they may buy a box of condoms at this late hour! Not very romantic! But then a coffin isn't very romantic, either!

But AIDS isn't caused by technological crimes against the environment, is it? Not as far as we know! Here the point may be irony: for all our much-vaunted technology, things have not changed so much from the primitive Middle Ages, since we are cringing in superstitious fear from the new plague as our ancestors did from the old. People today are saying AIDS is a scourge sent from God for our sins just as they said of the Bubonic Plague in medieval times. Only then the favorite scapegoat was Jews, whereas now it is Gays.

The actual damage done by heedless technology run riot comes in for consideration in the next lines. Acid rain sizzles on the forest floor while the blood-red tide licks the shores. Acid rain inevitably looms large in the awareness of lyricist Peart since Canada has a particular problem with it, thanks to the United States.

But not only does death rain from the skies, it waxes with the tides, as dangerous chemicals let loose directly into the sea by industrial waste ducts make history repeat itself yet again. Only this time the reference is perhaps to the Exodus story of Moses's plagues inflicted on Egypt. He waves his miracle-working staff and causes the precious water of the Nile to turn to blood. If there is any historical basis to the Moses story at all, the redness was caused by microscopic red flagella, but in any case the point is that the water was rendered undrinkable.

And we are calling essentially the same catastrophe down on our own heads!

Air pollution and the threadbare ozone layer come into view in the next stanza. Above us is a sky dripping poison, including fluorocarbons from aerosol spray cans. The poison in the air not only attacks us within, as we are forced to breathe it, but it fights us on a second front as well. Since fluorocarbons eat away at the ozone layer, more of the dangerous ultraviolet rays make it through what once was a protective screen, and increased risks of skin cancer are the result. You must now come in out of the sun because it only burns your skin. The atmosphere's threadbare and can no longer filter out the lethal radiation.

Environmental degradation of this magnitude is truly apocalyptic in scope, demonstrating the godlike, Promethean capacities of humanity. Think of it: we actually have it in our power to destroy the earth, to nullify the very safeguards set in place by nature. We may not in the long run prove ingenious enough to replace them with other protective measures, but no one can doubt our perverse greatness, as our collective epitaph will surely note.

Our destruction of the environment even transforms the archetypal, mythic feeling for nature. Whereas ancient men and women once blessed the sun and the rain as gifts of God, or even as gods themselves, we are coming to a day when the forces of nature, stripped of their wholesome aspect by the tampering hand of man, will come to be regarded instead as demonic powers inimical to human welfare. We can bless the sun and the rain no more. The ancient rivers were deified (the Jabbok in Israel, the Skamander in Troy, the Nile in Egypt) as beneficent life-givers, but who would ever think to divinize the modern-day Rhine, the Hudson, the Passaic? Each one runs like an open sore, like an open vein of AIDS-infected blood. They are cesspools in motion. Indeed, the ancient maxim of Heraclitus takes on a new meaning altogether: "You can't step into the same river twice"—because when you pull your foot out of the water after the first try, you only have left a smoking stump!

As the ever-increasing oil slicks spread in all directions, what do we see in the water but a spreading cloud of death, a black wind sinking to the ocean floor?

For a long while people neglected to trouble their heads over pollution. The world just seemed too big for that. The garbage was always going somewhere else. The world seemed wide enough to contain it somewhere conveniently and cosmetically out of sight. We still view outer space the same way: we don't think twice about all the space junk, rocket debris, etc., that we shoot into the Void, or simply leave endlessly orbiting there as an eternal monument to human wastefulness.

"Sure, dump the waste! Who cares? So long as it's not near *me*, so *my* kids aren't born mutants!"

But then—what do you know?—it turns out to be your neighborhood where they've decided to bury that radioactive waste! It rapidly becomes clear that the world isn't big enough for all the refuse we generate to be safely out of everyone's sight, out of everyone's mind.

What the ancient Psalmist said to God, we might say to the Grim Spectre of Pollution: "If I ascend into the sky, thou art there! If I make my bed in hell, thou art there! If I take the wings of the morning and fly to the uttermost parts of the sea, even there thy hand shall lead me" (Psalms 139:8-10). It is no more than a pipe dream to think, as some apparently do, that when things get bad enough we could just wash our hands of the mess we've made of planet Earth and hop aboard space ships and retreat to other planets. We don't even know for certain if there are any other worlds anywhere capable of supporting human life, and if there are, it would take many lifetimes to reach one, even traveling at the speed of light—which we can't do!

And what an irony, even if we could. Such an exodus would be the ultimate crowning gesture of *Homo sapiens* as heedless wasters: casting off a throw-away planet!

Our party is disrupted by an uninvited guest. In other words, "the party's over!" and it's time to pay the piper, to face the music for what we've done. Who is the uninvited guest? It is Doom personified. Two literary images come to mind at this point. To take the more ancient first, in Luke 17:26-30 we read of the end of the age arriving unexpectedly, not that there weren't signs of it to see if one were vigilant, but rather because people were heedless of their impending danger, just like today:

> As it was in the days of Noah, so will it be in the days
> of the Son of Man. They ate, they drank, they mar-
> ried, they were given in marriage, until the day that
> Noah entered the ark, and the flood came and de-
> stroyed them all. Likewise, as it was in the days of

> Lot—they ate, they drank, they bought, they sold, they planted, they built, but on the day when Lot went out from Sodom, fire and brimstone rained from the heaven and destroyed them all—so will it be on the day that the Son of Man is revealed.

The Son of Man comes as judge, jury, and executioner of the foolish human race. He is an uninvited and distinctly unwelcome guest. "For the Son of Man comes at an hour you do not expect" (Matthew 24:44).

The other literary parallel, and one perhaps more likely in Neil Peart's mind, in view of the imagery of the rest of the song, is that of Edgar Allan Poe's "The Masque of the Red Death." In this story, as the Red Death rages through the countryside, the nobility have taken refuge in the sumptuous palace of Prince Prospero. In gay abandonment they laugh sweetly but nervously, hoping to shut out the contagion and to ride out the storm till it should pass. But it is not to be so. One night amid a merry costume ball, a guest appears whom no one can quite identify. All are outraged at his poor taste, because his gaudy crimson finery denotes his pose as the Red Death incarnate, a bitter reminder of the plague from which they seek distraction. But the joke is still more bitter, as when the hour of unmasking strikes, it proves to be no disguise. And indeed, the party's over.

Remember how in "Second Nature" we saw depicted a mature attitude towards the Powers that be, a willingness to compromise replacing the obsolete absolutism of earlier songs (like "Closer to the Heart")? Here such *Realpolitik* has proven itself a dead end, since the Powers that be simply have too much power to need to compromise with anyone. Why should they? So "Red Tide" urges some kind of direct action. It's far too late for debate; the problem's too bad to ignore. The quiet rebellion of protest leads to open war. It's the eleventh hour if we want to turn the tide, that is, to turn the Red Tide away from our shore.

Does Peart have in view the controversial tactics of radical environmental groups like Earth First, who are willing to destroy equipment and even endanger human beings in order to retard the destruction of the environment? You'd have to ask him.

But something must be done. We can't simply acquiesce in the fate the corporate rapists have chosen for the planet. We are warned not to go gently into the endless winter night. This is an ecological adaptation of the title of Dylan Thomas's poem, "Do Not Go Gentle into That Good Night," which counsels not to yield passively to oncoming death. Its coming is never so inevitable that it cannot be forestalled for a few precious moments. And this advice is no less sound when it comes to the life that all of us share on this earth.

Why call the extinction of human life on a poisoned globe an endless winter night? Perhaps here we find a sidelong reference to yet another possible Doomsday scenario, that of the nuclear winter that some scientists have speculated might overtake the world following a full-scale nuclear war. It might be just the opposite: we could swelter to death in the wake of global warming and the Greenhouse Effect. But both dooms would be the backlash of the environment in response to the Frankenstein-like tampering of human ingenuity gone wild.

"Manhattan Project"

What was a haunting note of irony in "Red Tide"—the realization that it is precisely human greatness which makes possible the very obliteration of humanity itself!—becomes the predominant theme of "Manhattan Project" (*Power Windows*, 1985), a paean to the genius of the scientists who dared marshall the elemental power of the cosmos, atomic energy, for human use. The fact that the result was mass destruction at the time (shooting down the rising sun flag of Japan, as if the red dot in the center were a bull's eye target) and continual anxiety ever since (a nuclear neurosis that would hit everyone) is barely noticed in passing. Rush is scarcely indifferent to these matters, as "Red Tide" shows. We seem to have a depressing depiction, at least in part, of the aftermath of a nuclear war in "Red Sector A" (*Grace Under Pressure*, 1984), as the denizens of a Nazi-style concentration camp pine away, wondering if perhaps they may be the last ones left alive, the only human beings to survive.

But the focus in "Manhattan Project," as the very title (the code name of the scientific project that developed the A-Bomb) implies, is on the awesome wonder that human beings could effect so great a feat. Evil and tragic, perhaps; great with the hubris of fallen Lucifer, it may be, but great and Olympian nonetheless.

Had some other aspect of the birth and first use of the Atomic Bomb been the focus, surely the title would have been "Ground Zero" or "Shadows of the Blast," or whatever. Note the wistful awe of the refrain, how it bids us imagine a time, a man, a place where it all began. Rush stands in awe of the human greatness that could find the unseen atom, break it in human hands, those hands which had once swung from jungle vines, and unleash the force that causes suns to explode! Go to your anti-nuke rally if you want, foolishly trying to wish it away, but stop a minute first and gaze on the majesty of man who has wrought this thing, for good or for ill!

> What a piece of work is man!
> How noble in reason!
> How infinite in faculties!
> In form and moving how express and admirable!
> In action how like an angel!
> In apprehension how like a god!

The beauty of the world!
The paragon of animals!
    —(William Shakespeare, *Hamlet*)

Thanks to those humble bipeds, those mere hominids Oppenheimer and Einstein, the course of history would be changed for evermore.

"Countdown"

"Countdown" (*Signals*, 1982), an eyewitness account of the maiden launch of the space shuttle Columbia in 1981, brings home the same point, though with a less controversial example, that of space flight.

Some political radicals will place the rocket alongside the Atomic Bomb as an instrument of mass death, since they deem the space program a superfluous distraction from the urgent business of feeding the welfare state. If the A-Bomb killed millions quickly by nuclear firestorm, the space rocket starves them slowly by its diversion of needed funds, or so some say. But Rush would certainly deem such carpers, to use Lovecraft's phrase, "self-blinded earth-gazers."

Both the lyrics and the music for "Countdown" are alive with the pulsebeat of what Lovecraft called "adventurous expectancy." The song is not so much a comment on the moment as it is an attempt to recreate it for the listener. Rush seeks to conjure up a magic day when super technology will mingle with the bright stuff of dreams. Again, as negatively in "Red Tide," here we see a positive reference to the ability of human ingenuity to realize the mythic. There it was a case of reversing the archetypes, as sun and rain were changed by human device from benign deities to avenging demons. Here, however, it is as if the dragon, that great symbol of the elemental force of earth, were brought to life by the hand of man: the waiting rocket, straining at the leash, is venting vapours, like the breath of a snoring ivory dragon.

This song is full of awe, like the awe at a sacred revelation or at a stupendous spectacle of nature. But it is neither which provokes such gaping marvel; rather the achievement of humanity! The very words of the song trail off, lost in astonishment.

Let's not leave the image of a sacred epiphany too quickly. In it we can trace yet another common thread connecting "Countdown" with "Manhattan Project." After the launch of the space rocket, we find a description of a pillar of cloud, the smoke that lingers high in the air. We cannot but be reminded of the image, in "Manhattan Project," of the ascending mushroom cloud implicit in the description of the big bang that shook the world. Surely in both cases we catch an allusion to the epiphany of Jehovah in the Book of Exodus, when he appeared as a pillar of fire by night and a pillar of cloud by day (Exodus 13:22). What we are seeing in both these songs is an epiphany of the godlike power of the human mind, and of its manifestation in the physical world, technology, the cutting edge, the leading edge of life.

In a segment of *Bill Moyers's World of Ideas*, Jacob Needleman, a philosopher and writer on mysticism, recounted an experience very similar to that chronicled in "Countdown." Needleman had been invited to witness the launch of Apollo 17. He recalls,

> We were sitting on the lawn, drinking beer and waiting for this huge white thing, at night, illuminated, looking like a religious [spire? monolith? idol?]...this tall, 35 story high, white rocket, lit by these powerful lamps, and we were all sitting around, joking, wise-cracking...and the countdown came.... There was the usual delay, and we were all waiting and waiting and waiting.
>
> And then comes this launch. And the first thing you see is this extraordinary orange light, which is just at the limit of the light that you can bear to look at.... It's beautiful; everything's illuminated with this light. Then comes this slow thing rising up. Total silence, because it takes a few seconds for the sound to come across. And then comes this *hummmmmm-mmm*. It enters right into you.
>
> And this extraordinary thing is lifting up. And then everybody, all these cynical people,...these wise-cracking people, myself included—suddenly you could practically hear jaws dropping. "O my God...." And the sense of wonder fills everyone in the whole place as this thing goes up and up and up and up. And then the first stage ignites, and this beautiful blue flame...and it becomes like a star. And you realize there are human beings on it.
>
> And then total silence, and people just get up and quietly help each other up, ...looking at each other, speaking quietly and interestedly. These were suddenly moral people. Because wonder, the sense of wonder, the experience of wonder had made them moral. By the time we got to the hotel, it was gone!

Needleman counts this as one of those experiences where your usually dormant Self suddenly wakes up. You know you are alive, not merely on automatic pilot. In those moments you are summoned to full attention by the revelation of something so surpassingly great that it takes you out of yourself and lifts you up towards higher possibilities, toward a greater fulfillment of latent human capabilities.

Rush seems to have learned the same lesson from the same experience. We will see shortly how for Rush technology is so much an extension of human nature that it may actually function as a symbol of human nature. Here we have a reversal of the kind of human-machine imagery we found in "The Body Electric." There the idea was that human beings may be reduced to the degraded condition of mere drones. But here we see the greatest products of human genius used metonymously to stand for the genius that created them, as in Genesis chapter one, where the creation bears the divine image of the creator.

"Red Barchetta"

With "Red Barchetta" (*Moving Pictures*, 1981) we have entered Rush's time machine and returned to a dystopia reminiscent of that in the earlier "2112," an imagined future where collective squeamishness has put the damper on any individual excellence or adventuresomeness. An exaggerated concern for safety has apparently led to the banning of all individual motor travel. Mass transit is the only transit allowed to good, sheeplike citizens. "The Motor Law" has long since put an end to both traffic accidents and exhaust pollution.

The song's story opens with our hero, an unnamed throwback with an atavistic streak of individualism and a thirst for excitement, surreptitiously jumping aboard a freight train, hobo style, to hitch a ride over an otherwise guarded border into the countryside, evidently a place he is not supposed to go, outside his urban hive. There his uncle maintains a clandestine retreat amid the apparent ruins of a farm. There are no more farms in the forbidden countryside, replaced, one may guess, by hydroponic collective farms somewhere within the protective dome of the City (the twin, no doubt, of the one we visited in "The Body Electric"). The farm has been obsolete since the Motor Law made the ownership and operation of individual farm vehicles a crime.

But our protagonist manages now and then to sneak away to the country retreat which even in its decline serves as a reminder of a better, vanished time, much as the dusty little antique shop does for Winston Smith in *Nineteen Eighty-Four*. It is now as illegal as the vehicles that once would have taken one there on the open roads under a sunny sky. No one knows about it, or it would be destroyed. And there in the seeming wreckage of a half-collapsed barn such as one sees along the county roads of any rural area, there lies hidden, under a pile of camouflage debris, an even more remarkable relic of the cherished past: a gleaming red antique, a Barchetta sports car. It corresponds to the old guitar discovered in "2112."

Somehow the protagonist's uncle has managed to keep the car in fine running shape, no mean feat in a society where auto parts must be as contraband as autos. But he has been willing to take the trouble: it is his silent rebellion against the oppression of the modern age. He

dares not even drive it, not wishing to be apprehended by the ever-vigilant authorities ("the Eyes"), who patrol the roads like buzzards looking for road-kill carrion—which is very likely what he would become if
they caught him!

But the nephew has not even the memory of the open roads, so
he braves the wrath of the authorities and ventures forth onto the sterile
roads, empty, of course, of all traffic. To sit behind the wheel of the
forbidden car is to sit at the controls of a time machine. To speed along
the deserted highway is in truth to speed back in time to the era in
which the car was at home.

We must suppose his uncle had taught him, purely in theory,
how to drive, in the quiet of the ruined barn. But he is confident of his
abilities as he opens the throttle: the wind streams through his hair.
He shifts gears, lets the car drift as its perfect humming engine makes
its mechanical music. His own adrenalin surges as if he'd just floored
some biological gas pedal. He is driving drunk, intoxicated by the
scented country air (it would seem, at least, that the Motor Law was effective in curbing pollution!) and the brilliant reflection of the sunlight
on chrome. The landscape becomes a blur speeding past him. He is
alive as never before, every nerve humming.

This joy ride is his weekly crime, but somehow he has always
managed to evade the patrols—until now! Suddenly, ahead of him,
rounding the curve of the mountain road, appears a gleaming metal air-
car, making right for him. It is wider than his Barchetta, designed to
hog both lanes of the road which its air cushion skirts, in order to trap
oncoming cars. All he can do is to spin around, tires shrieking, and try
to evade the patrol. But a second appears out of nowhere as soon as it
becomes clear to the pursuers that the living fossil Barchetta still has
some life in her and doesn't plan to give up without a run for the
money!

If adrenalin surged before, it floods now! He drives like the
wind, testing the limits of machine and man alike. Laughing aloud
from the hormonal rush ("The Outsider's salvation lies in extremes"—Colin Wilson), he fashions a desperate plan. He thought he'd
noticed a one-lane bridge somewhere along the road—yes, there it
is—just enough room for his car to pass, but hopeless for the giant vehicles, who stop stranded like a frustrated pack of hounds eluded by a
fox. He races back to the farm to rejoin his uncle dreaming safe at the
fireside.

But wait a minute! Surely more patrols would be on their way
to scour the countryside, and it could not take them long to discover the
farm, still inhabited in this forbidden zone. Why is the driver so safe
and secure? It can only be because the preceding race against the authorities in the ancient car was itself a fireside dream of rebellion. Perhaps as his uncle retraces those roads in memory, his nephew joins him

in imagination. Was it a road race in reverie only, such as the listener experiences? This, too, is a form of quiet rebellion.

"Red Barchetta" is another Randian protest against the rule of enforced mediocrity and cloying collective safety. But our principle interest in it here is the use it makes, again, of technology as a symbol for human nature, human craftsmanship, creativity, and daring. Really, the Barchetta sports car stands for the daring spirit of the nephew. It stands for the vitality, as well as the superior standards, of an earlier day, before human nature was degraded by the leaden weights of modernity and mediocrity.

It is a shining example of what life could be: full of beauty, energy, and joy. And though it is to a great extent the plague of Industrialism that has killed the human soul, transforming us into androids, technology was only the tool in the hands of those who used it to build a prison for the fearful, the Mass-Production Zone.

If we find ourselves to be among the cringing denizens of that Zone, we have ourselves to blame. We must clench our plastic fists and make for the controls of that Barchetta. If technology was used to imprison us, it can equally be the key to our liberation. The right hands have to be at the controls, those of the New World Man.

Consider the difference between the images of the android in "The Body Electric" and the man driving the sports car in "Red Barchetta." The first is man mechanized; the second is machine humanized. In "Red Barchetta," the car is one, symbolically, with the liberated human being. The sensations of the driver mix impressions of car and driver indiscriminately: mechanical music, adrenalin surge, old leather, hot metal and oil, etc.

The same image can be found in Stanley G. Weinbaum's novel of the evolutionary superman, *The New Adam* (1939). In this science fiction classic, the next stage of human evolution arrives on the scene. His name is Edmond Hall. His life among his half-asleep inferiors (us!) is a long experiment in relieving boredom. One of his few satisfactions is driving his beloved grey roadster.

> Machines...were to him simply extensions of his body; impulses flowed as easily through his limbs to the thrusting wheels on the road as to his finger tips. He and the vehicle moved as a single being.... He drove the machine with almost miraculous dexterity, slipping through traffic like wind through grain...and the thrill of driving was as if he used his own muscles. Sometimes he drove to the open country, selecting unpatrolled dirt roads, and here drove at breath-taking speed, pitting his skill against the vagaries of the terrain.

The image is essentially the same, that of the individual who, for whatever reason, has not succumbed to the numbing mediocrity of the mundane herd around him. He finds his own excellence expressed and mirrored in a mechanical device. As it soars effortlessly through the landscape, so does the Outsider glide through the torpid crowds who drift aimlessly and without real energy or direction. In the flawless precision of the well-tuned automobile, he recognizes the image of his own balance and integrity.

> Each machine has its own, unique personality which probably could be defined as the intuitive sum total of everything you know and feel about it. This personality constantly changes, usually for the worse, but sometimes surprisingly for the better, and it is this personality that is the real object of motorcycle maintenance.
> The real cycle you're working on is a cycle called yourself.
> Working on a motorcycle, working well, caring, is to become part of a process, to achieve an inner peace of mind.

So says Robert M. Pirsig in *Zen and the Art of Motorcycle Maintenance*. "The motorcycle is primarily a mental phenomenon." So, we would suggest, is the red Barchetta.

"Natural Science"

If technology is the mirror of human greatness, it can also be (to use Christopher Woodforde's phrase) "the mirror of man's damnation." In "Natural Science" (*Permanent Waves*, 1980) we press in closer to the heart of the problem with technology, as well as to the solution for that problem. Both depend upon technology as the mirror reflection of man himself.

The song first asks us to imagine the string of short-lived island universes left behind when the tide goes out. In the rocky crags are trapped small pockets of water and tiny sea-life. Instantly each pool has become a private cosmos, as isolated as if it were the only little ecosystem in existence. It will soon be swept back to the relative oblivion of boundless union with the great ocean from which it so recently sprang. But for the time being, the tiny creatures who swim in it may be forgiven for thinking themselves supreme in the universe.

Their tenuous and solipsistic existence is a simple sort of mirror reflecting our own microcosm. Indeed, implicit in the song is that in the swirling tempest-in-a-teapot cosmos of the tidal pools, we are seeing a mirror of the humble origins of all earthly life. The egocentric arrogance born there will stay with us like a controlling strand of DNA throughout human history, putting its unfortunate stamp on all our endeavors.

Vedanta Hinduism uses the same striking image. Shankara taught that what appears to us, in our state of ignorance, to be our own individual ego, unconquerable and indomitable, is actually a tiny drop of water cast up for a moment by a wave crashing against the shore. Given another moment, that drop will fall back to rejoin the universal ocean of consciousness from which it had momentarily imagined itself separated. But, as long as we cling to the illusion of arrogant individuality, we delay the joyous reunion with the *rest* of us, the single Cosmic Self, the All.

Next, in a breathtaking historical sweep reminiscent of the movie *2001: A Space Odyssey*, when the film jumps from the dawn of apish intelligence all the way to space travel, the song takes us a quantum leap forward in time and space where we are horrified to behold a mechanized world careening out of control. Born of human genius, yet gone wrong with our arrogance, it evidences both triumph and tragedy, a mix of mess and magic, the mess of "Red Tide" and the magic of "Countdown." Like the narcotized amusement park in Huxley's *Brave New World*, the world has become a computer-driven clinic for a cynical elite who dance to a synthetic band—Digital Men, in short.

No one meant it all to turn out this way; no one is born a Digital Man, an android. It was all quite unforeseen. Just like the living motes in that primordial tidal pool, we simply cannot see the big picture, that our actions (such as dumping pollution and eroding the ozone layer) are not hermetically self-contained but have far-reaching repercussions. Our choices make ripples in the surface of our ocean which travel much, much farther than the tiny tidal pool's worth of reality we can see.

It is not as if science in itself were some corruptire force, like the Ring of Power in Tolkien's *The Lord of the Rings*. The problem is rather that we have created our science and technology in our own image (what else could we do, after all?). It is a mirror and extension of our nature. And though we may conquer nature in the world outside us, we cannot seem to subdue our own human nature.

If we could, then maybe we could solve, or better yet, avert, these problems. A purified human nature would then express itself in a purified science. Like nature, science too must be tamed. If it is not, then both science and nature (at least human nature) will be lost. Wave after wave will flow with the tide of cosmic evolution, which even pretentious humanity cannot confute, and bury the world as it does. One tide will follow another inexorably, receding to leave life, in whatever new forms may evolve, to go on as before.

The sole shred of hope offered in the generally gloomy song is that somehow a very different product and mirror of human nature may temper and soften runaway, soulless technology. That unlikely-seeming savior is art. Whence this solution? We must seek the explanation in the next song. But "Natural Science" provides the clue: they don't grasp what's happening because the world has been created in their own image. External nature and our own human nature are of a piece, neither easily understandable. There is no hope of reforming human nature, and thus its products, as long as human nature remains a mystery to us.

"Hemispheres"

"Hemispheres" (*Hemispheres*, 1978) is an allegory about human nature set in the form of a creation myth which utilizes the gods of Greek mythology. The story recounts successive, rival efforts of the gods Apollo and Dionysus to provide guidance for the fledgling human race. Each offers his own brand of wisdom, Apollo that of efficient, calculating reason, Dionysus that of instinctual, chaotic ecstasy. Each has its advantages, but each leaves dangerous blind spots, as well as needs unmet.

At length, with the world torn in half, into hollow hemispheres, a balance is struck. It is decided that both wisdoms are needed, each being quite indispensable, and the crucial thing is to know when which ought to come into play. The deity Cygnus steps forth to offer this, the most important wisdom of all. All is right with the world, or at least things are now off to a more hopeful start.

Apollo and Dionysus have long been literary and philosophical symbols for the rational and the instinctual aspects of human nature, and it is no secret that this is their allegorical function in this song. It is plain that the struggle going on here between Apollo and Dionysus is transpiring in the individual human psyche: every soul is a battlefield. Each spirit was split into hollow hemispheres but at length reconciled, heart and mind united in a single perfect sphere. The cover of the album is a dead giveaway, depicting the two hemispheres of a naked brain. Perched on each is a miniature figure. A prim and officious-looking businessman, briefcase in hand, stands straight as an arrow atop one half, a live and limber ballet dancer spins atop the other. In short, we are in the realm, not just of philosophical abstraction, but of brain physiology.

In recent years brain research has progressed to the point where scientists now feel confident of having locally isolated certain functions of the brain. Ironically, we are accustomed to laughing at the "primitive" notions of ancient and native peoples who located certain virtues and emotions in this or that part of the body. Now we find they were a lot closer to the truth than our arrogance allowed us to see. It turns out that we *can* map where to find certain functions of the soul in the body.

They are to be found, not as far flung throughout the body as the ancients imagined, but distributed nonetheless, between the left and right hemispheres of the brain. This was first suggested by research on so-called "split-brain" patients, those whose brain hemispheres had been separated because of epileptic seizures. Experiments demonstrated that each half of the brain was virtually a self-sufficient, self-contained brain in and of itself, each with its own perceptual and memory systems. A split-brain patient was found not to be able to write down with his left hand what he had seen with his right eye, and vice versa! If, as is normally the case, the two brains work in tandem, there is no such isolation. Each brain informs the other of what it learns.

It appears that each side of the brain has a certain specialty. The left brain is analytical, verbal, logical, adept at math. The right brain is not much good at these things, but in it reside creativity, insight, vitality, and emotion. In other words, Apollo lives in the left hemisphere, Dionysus in the right.

In some people the right brain predominates. They will be more affective and emotional, more attuned to the arts. And they may very likely be left-handed, since each side of the brain controls the motor functions of the opposite side of the body. In other people the left side predominates, and they are more likely to be adept at math, science, logic, and so on.

Some have suggested that "nerdism" is a result of someone being heavily left-brained: they are powerful in the intellectual realm, but with no esthetic sense whatever, and thus with no consciousness of how they appear to others!

The division of functions between the halves of the brain does not mean simply that one side of the brain takes over for certain jobs, making way for the other when its specialty is needed. It is a bit more complicated than that. You really need both working together, at least for some tasks.

In one of his writings on the subject, *The Laurel and Hardy Theory of Consciousness*, Colin Wilson suggests that the right brain supplies the vitality and energy for whatever the left brain does. One cannot easily do intellectual work without a sense of enthusiasm or momentum. The left brain supplies the first, the right brain the second. Also, as all writers know, the lucid and persuasive expression of one's ideas is easier if the creativity is flowing. It flows, when and if it does, from the right brain. So if you intend to write a clear and persuasive account of your ideas, you'd better have both sides of the brain running smoothly at the same time.

The real pioneer of split-brain psychology is Sir Julian Jaynes, author of *The Origin of Consciousness in the Breakdown of the Bicameral Mind*. In this book he suggested that in earlier ages, when the two sides of the brain were on somewhat less familiar terms with one another, the voice of one brain hemisphere communicating with the other actually seemed like hearing the voice of God, or of a spirit, or of the Muse inside one's head. The biblical prophets, for example, were really listening to the thundering oracles of their own right brains (as is craftily suggested in the Charlton Heston movie *The Ten Commandments*, where the voice speaking to Moses at the Burning Bush, if you listen carefully, is Moses's own!). Remember what we said about the harsh taskmaster of artistic inspiration in the previous chapter. It is perhaps the right brain feeding too-powerful inspiration to the left brain!

Wilson theorizes that the reason we have so much trouble at so many things is that the left brain underestimates the great, perhaps even unthinkable, potential of the right brain and so chokes off that potential. Why do we use so small a proportion of our mental capacity? Perhaps, Wilson theorizes, because we just do not imagine we can utilize any more! To borrow some notions from elsewhere in Wilson's work, we can imagine that it would be the true Outsider, that member of the elite "Five Percent" who have "Faculty X," who is best able to use the left brain to marshall the great power of the right brain.

It was surely some instinctive insight rather than a wild guess that led Weinbaum to conceive his evolutionary superman, Edmond Hall, as he did. For one of his greatest gifts is the New Adam's fully functional double brain. In Edmond Hall, both hemispheres had developed to the point that each was actually capable of simultaneous, independent functioning! We first discover this in an early scene, where we see young Edmond in school, chastened by the teacher for gazing out the window:

> "Edmond Hall!" was her impatient exclamation. "Please forget that window and pay attention!" This followed with the most surprising statement he had heard during his seven school years. "No one can think of two things at once!" Edmond knew she was wrong. He *had* been following her. For he himself could with perfect clarity pursue two separate and distinct trains of thought at the same time.

As *The New Adam* progresses, Edmond undergoes a great struggle over the question of the role of passion in his life. He seems designed primarily for pure intellection. Indeed, there is no scientific problem he cannot solve. But he cannot seem to slough off the last vestiges of the human instinct for love and lust. And thereby hangs this most interesting tale. In a sense his dilemma is a replaying of the primordial struggle between Apollo and Dionysus in every human soul.

And though "Hemispheres" gives that struggle a happy ending, it is far from clear that Cygnus has yet made her appearance. Isn't it precisely for her absence that the future world of "Natural Science" is a mechanized world that's gotten out of hand?

It is in the difference between the brain hemispheres, and the products of each, that we can perhaps find the perspective from which to unravel what might at first seem the most glaring of contradictions in Rush's lyrics. On the one hand, do we not find running throughout their songs a strong emphasis on reason and a contempt for those who abdicate it? For example, Rush scoffs at superstitious people who pay heed to celestial voices to make their difficult decisions for them instead of thinking for themselves ("Free Will"). It is only one small step from such emotion- (or fear-) ruled know-nothingism to full-fledged bigotry, painted in lurid hues in "Witch Hunt."

Yet on the other hand, Rush bids us to move as fast as we can closer to the heart. The several songs which envision a futuristic scientific dystopia, *à la Brave New World*, are warnings that rationalism may get out of hand and squeeze out the human spirit. People become mere androids, scarcely capable of lifting a plastic fist in defiance.

Science is the villain in songs like these, yet then what are we to make of "Countdown," where the ascending rocket seems to symbolize the ascent of the human spirit to a whole new realm of evolution? Even the hated atomic mushroom cloud becomes an epiphany of human genius in "Manhattan Project," as we have already seen. What's going on here?

We should take our clue from the moment recounted in "Countdown" when super-science mixes with the potent stuff of dreams. That is the moment of Cygnus, the dawn of a new perspective which transcends both brain hemispheres of logic and instinct and fuses them into some higher synthesis.

And here we have to mention the philosophy of Romanticism. Rush, as we have seen, is not much concerned to sing about romance, at least in the sense that dominates almost all other rock and popular songs. Rush would much rather sing, and Peart would rather write, about ideas. But there is a sense in which Rush and their songs are the essence of Romanticism.

This is the name of an aesthetic and philosophical movement that arose toward the end of the eighteenth century and flourished in the nineteenth. It was a reaction to the dry Rationalistic philosophy of Descartes, Spinoza, and Leibniz. To be fair, these thinkers certainly left some space for the non-rational side of human experience, but they did think reason was the most important key for understanding reality and our place in it.

They reasoned that reality was capable of being explained according to a kind of mathematical or even grammatical analysis. Everything was a deduction from certain innate ideas. And this way of looking at things is obviously a big improvement on using blind faith, superstition, and the dead weight of tradition as your guide to living.

Or, to put it another way, Apollo's wisdom is genuine wisdom, light that illumines the darkness. But it is a light in which one can only see certain things. We still need Dionysus.

There is a scene in one of Michael Moorcock's Elric novels in which the hero, last heir of the line of sorcerer kings of ancient Melniboné, has a vision of the future, the future which would come to exist if the forces of Order were ever to triumph completely over those of Chaos. It is a sterile realm of static perfection—and death. If order is complete, there can be no room left for the unpredictable bit of chaos we call life.

Such seemed the danger of Rationalism, and the Romantics reacted with alarm. Immanuel Kant tried to set a limit beyond which reason dared not transgress. His point was not that one must rein in reason when it could go further, given the chance. What he meant was that there is a genuine limit to reason, namely the limit of sense perception. The thinker will get into deep trouble if he or she tries to use reason with no sense data to go on. Then one winds up with unverifiable fantasies. But where reason cannot take us, intuition can.

Kant admitted that we cannot, as the Rationalists thought we could, know anything about God or the afterlife with any certainty. But do we stop dead there, unable to prove life has any moral meaning, whether there is any justice in the world? No, we do not, Kant said. We are faced with a decision about what we are going to make of life. It is not merely some intellectual conundrum which we could afford to leave unsolved.

Are we really prepared to say that since science cannot show us there is any verifiable meaning, or that there is a divine Judge and Lawgiver, that we will remain content with a paralyzing agnosticism on these questions? Are we really prepared to admit that our moral conscience may be sheer illusion? That there are no objective moral standards? Granted science and reason cannot provide any.

So what are we to do? We may make, not a rational inference, but a moral one, an instinctive inference, a step of faith, that there is a moral truth resident in the universe. Sure, we can't prove it, but we need it to be true, and it would make a lot of sense of things if it were true.

Kant called it "practical reason," a faculty of transcending the realm of strict fact and reason, based on the recognition that there are realms of life which just do not work by those rules. In one way or another, all the Romantics tried to make this point. They were calling in Cygnus to mediate the dispute between the warring hemispheres of Apollo and Dionysus.

Another factor that motivated them was the increasingly depressing effects of the Industrial Revolution. The skies were getting blacker, the world was uglier and meaner, what with sweat shops, slave-driven assembly lines, and the generally tawdrier complexion of life. Romanticism, by contrast, stressed the beauty in life, the sensitivities for which burgeoning Capitalism no longer had time. The Romantics wanted to preserve and safeguard the artistic and emotional quality of life against soulless science and industry. Romanticism was the first protest against the Mass-Production Zone, the first call to come closer to the heart.

Yet Romanticism was not some implausible primitivism, not like the Luddites, who protested against scientific industrialism by smashing every machine they could get their hands on. Such an effort was foredoomed to failure. The machine, one might say, is like the stone in the proverb: whoever kicks it will be sorry, and if it falls on him he will be crushed. The Romantics were not so naive. As seen most clearly in the philosophy of Hegel, the Romantics embraced the notions of change and inevitable progress. Some Romantics, like Schopenhauer, were pessimistic, influenced by the anti-worldliness of Buddhism, but most were quite optimistic. As long as the reins of reason were the strings of the heart, change would be progress to a greater and brighter future. Technology could be the friend of the human spirit, not the enslaver of it. Technology frees us to have more time for intellectual and artistic experiments. And, of course, machines can facilitate artistic experiences, as you know by the sheer fact of being able to listen to Rush on your CD player. As Josef Pieper summed it up in the title of his book, *Leisure* [is] *the Basis of Culture.*

Hegel saw history as a vast sweep of change: one idea or state of affairs would for a time clash with an opposing one, and then the difference between the two would be somehow transcended in a new synthesis of both, higher than either. In other words, he knows no changes are permanent, but change is.

You can see, then, that when Rush hymns the achievements of technology as a triumph of the human spirit, it is because super-science has mingled with the bright stuff of dreams. Cygnus has reconciled the hemispheres. When Rush places us amid the desolation of Red Sector A or the Mass-Production Zone, they are warning of the possible triumph of Apollo and the extermination of Dionysus.

Perhaps Cygnus is another name for Weinbaum's New Adam, a new kind of human with competent use of both sides of the brain. Only such a species of New Adams and Eves, of New World Men and Women, will be able to temper cold reason with warm insight, objective science with subjective art. Perhaps only then will the androids become fully human.

VIII.

CONCLUSION: NOT LOOKING BACK

This book has discussed several major interlocking themes in the lyrics of Rush: courage, individualism, persistence, reason, and the heart. The same themes continue to echo through the later albums of Rush, not treated here. Obviously, the only way a book like this can be up-to-date and completely comprehensive is to deal with a group whose work is finished. Fortunately, Rush is still going strong, and, one hopes, will continue to outdistance any book anyone writes about them. I venture to say, however, that the appearance of more Rush songs does not render *Mystic Rhythms* obsolete. Neil Peart's approach to the issues discussed here does not seem to change in any important way in the more recent songs. We have seen how songs may be cited from various older and more recent albums interchangably, according to theme. This in now way implies that the songs in questions are redundant; to the contrary, they simply approach the same themes from different angles, enhancing one another. No doubt the newer songs present even more complementary approaches, but the basic things, I think, have been said. Thus, to slavishly comb the songs from *Roll the Bones*, *Counterparts*, and *Test for Echo* would risk making this book redundant.

On the other hand, these new albums do break new paths, explore new ideas, impressions, and questions. There are not only new treatments of old themes; there are new themes altogether. For instance, *Counterparts* is occupied with questions of male-female roles, Jungian archetypes, paganism, Girardian "mimetic desire," and others. *Roll the Bones* invokes the ghost of Fritz Leiber and his story, "Gonna Roll the Bones," and alludes to a number of current philosophical debates, most importantly, Postmodernism and Deconstruction. The latter provides a toehold for the application of a whole new arsenal of critical approaches to the lyrics of Rush themselves. Postmodernism casts new light on earlier songs, especially "Mystic Rhythms." And Rush's preoccupation with technology, its promise and pitfalls, as well as the way technology both mirrors and shapes human nature, surfaces again in *Test for Echo*. This time, however, the emphasis has shifted, because technology itself has shifted, from manufacturing (the "Mass-Production Zone") to service and information ("net boy, net girl").

All these themes and more deserve an extensive treatment of their own. The songs must not be whittled down to fit, like square pegs in round holes, into the thematic categories of this book. I intend to pursue a separate discussion of the ideas hinted at in this conclusion in the sequel to the present volume. If Rush can keep on creating, so can I!

A RUSH DISCOGRAPHY

1974 *Rush.* Finding My Way, Need Some Love, Take a Friend, Here Again, What You're Doing, In the Mood, Before and After, Working Man. Mercury/PolyGram 822 541-2 M-1.

1975 *Fly by Night.* Anthem, Best I Can, Beneath, Between and Behind, By-Tor and the Snow Dog, Fly by Night, Making Memories, Rivendell, In the End. Mercury/PolyGram 822 542-2 M-1.

1975 *Caress of Steel.* Bastille Day, I Think I'm Going Bald, Lakeside Park, The Necromancer (includes Into the Darkness, Under the Shadow, Return of the Prince), The Fountain of Lamneth (includes In the Valley, Didacts and Narpets, No One at the Bridge, Panacea, Bacchus Plateau, The Fountain). Mercury/ PolyGram 822 543-2 M-1.

1975 *Archives.* Reissue of first three albums as a three-record set. Polydor 822 553.

1976 *2112.* 2112 (includes Overture, The Temples of Syrinx, Discovery, Presentation, Oracle: The Dream, Soliloquy, Grand Finale), A Passage to Bangkok, The Twilight Zone, Lessons, Tears, Something for Nothing. Mercury/PolyGram 822 545-2 M-1.

1976 *All the World's a Stage.* Two-record set: live performance of Bastille Day, Anthem, Fly by Night, In the Mood, Something for Nothing, Lakeside Park, 2112 (includes Overture, The Temples of Syrinx, Presentation, Soliloquy, Grand Finale), By-Tor and the Snow Dog, In the End, Working Man, Finding My Way, What You're Doing. Mercury/PolyGram 822 552-2 M-1.

1977 *A Farewell to Kings.* A Farewell to Kings, Xanadu, Closer to the Heart, Cinderella Man, Madrigal, Cygnus X-1. Mercury/PolyGram 822 546-2 M-1.

1978 *Hemispheres.* Cygnus X-1 Book II Hemispheres (includes Prelude, Apollo/Dionysus, Armageddon, Cygnus, The Sphere), Circumstances, The Trees, La Villa Strangiato. Mercury/PolyGram 822 547-2 M-1.

1980 *Permanent Waves.* The Spirit of Radio, Freewill, Jacob's Ladder, Entre Nous, Different Strings, Natural Science. Mercury/PolyGram 822 548-2 M-1.

1981   *Moving Pictures*. Tom Sawyer, Red Barchetta, YYZ, Limelight, The
        Camera Eye, Witch Hunt, Vital Signs. Mercury/PolyGram 800 048-
        2.

1981   *Exit...Stage Left*. Live performance of The Spirit of Radio, Red
        Barchetta, YYZ, A Passage to Bangkok, Closer to the Heart, Be-
        neath, Between and Behind, Jacob's Ladder, Broon's Bane, The
        Trees, Xanadu, Freewill, Tom Sawyer, La Villa Strangiato. Mer-
        cury/PolyGram 822 551-2 M-1.

1982   *Signals*. Subdivisions, The Analog Kid, Chemistry, Digital Man, The
        Weapon, New World Man, Losing It, Countdown. Mer-
        cury/PolyGram 810 002-2.

1984   *Grace Under Pressure*. Distant Early Warning, Afterimage, Red Sec-
        tor A, the Enemy Within, The Body Electric, Kid Gloves, Red
        Lenses, Between the Wheels. Mercury/PolyGram 818 476-2.

1985   *Power Windows*. The Big Money, Grand Designs, Manhattan Project,
        Marathon, Territories, Middletown Dreams, Emotion Detector,
        Mystic Rhythms. Mercury/PolyGram 826 098-2 M-1.

1986   *Rushhour*. Live performance (Toronto, 1986) of The Spirit of Radio,
        The Enemy Within, Witch Hunt, New World Man, Distant Early
        Warning, Red Sector A, Closer to the Heart, Tom Sawyer, Lime-
        light, Finding My Way, In the Mood. Spotlight SL—CD 009.

1987   *Hold Your Fire*. Force Ten, Time Stand Still, Open Secrets, Second
        Nature, Prime Mover, Lock and Key, Mission, Turn the Page, Tai
        Shan, High Water. Mercury/PolyGram 832 464-2 Q-1

1989   *A Show of Hands*. Live perfomance of Intro, The Big Money, Subdivi-
        sions, Marathon, Turn the Page, Manhattan Project, Mission, Distant
        Early Warning, Mystic Rhythms, Witch Hunt, The Rhythm Method,
        Force Ten, Time Stand Still, Red Sector A, Closer to the Heart.
        Mercury/PolyGram 836 346-2.

1989   *Presto*. Show Don't Tell, Chain Lightning, The Pass, War Paint,
        Scars, Presto, Superconductor, Anagram, Red Tide, Hand Over Fist,
        Available Light. Anthem/Atlantic 7 82040-2.

1990   *Chronicles*. Compilation of previously released recordings of Finding
        My Way, Working Man, Fly by Night, Anthem, Bastille Day, Lake-
        side Park, 2112, (includes Overture, The Temples of Syrinx), What
        You're Doing (live), A Farewell to Kings, Closer to the Heart, The
        Trees, La Villa Strangiato, Freewill, The Spirit of Radio, Tom
        Sawyer, Red Barchetta, Limelight, A Passage to Bangkok (live),
        Subdivisions, New World Man, Distant Early Warning, Red Sector
        A, The Big Money, Manhattan Project, Force Ten, Time Stand Still,
        Mystic   Rhythms   (live),   Show   Don't   Tell.   An-
        them/Mercury/PolyGram 838 936-2.

1991   *The Fly*. Live performance (Madison Square Garden, December 7,
        1991) of Force Ten, Limelight, Freewill, Distant Early Warning,

Time Stand Still, Dreamline, Bravado, Roll the Bones, Show Don't Tell, The Big Money, Ghost of a Chance, Subdivisions, The Pass. PIXEL Studio.

1991 *Life Under Pressure*. Live performance (Civic Arena, Pittsburgh, July 8, 1984) of The Spirit of Radio, The Enemy Within, Witch Hunt, New World Man, Distant Early Warning, Red Sector A, Closer to the Heart, Tom Sawyer, Freewill, Finding My Way. Metal Memory MM 90021.

1991 *Roll the Bones*. Dreamline, Bravado, Roll the Bones, Face Up, Where's My Thing?, The Big Wheel, Heresy, Ghost of a Chance, Neurotica, You Bet Your Life. Anthem/Atlantic 7 82293-2.

1991 *Rushian Roulette*. Live performance (Pink Pop Festival, Geleen, Holland, May, 1979) of A Passage to Bangkok, Xanadu, The Trees, Closer to the Heart, La Villa Strangiato, 2112 (part 2), In the Mood, Something for Nothing. Metal Memory 90018.

1992 *Bravado*. Two-disc set: live performance (Nassau Coliseum, March 15, 1992) of Force Ten, Limelight, Freewill/Distant Early Warning, Time Stand Still, Dreamline, Bravado, Roll the Bones, Show Don't Tell, The Big Money, Ghost of a Chance, Subdivisions, The Pass, Where's My Thing?, Drum Solo, Closer to the Heart, Xanadu/Superconductor, Tom Sawyer, The Spirit of Radio, Overture/Finding My Way/La Villa Strangiato/Anthem/Red Barchetta. Red Robin Records 06.

1992 *Fly in the Night*. Live performance (Montreal, 1980) of Intro/Xanadu, A Farewell to Kings, Closer to the Heart, Something for Nothing, Cygnus X-1, Working Man, Fly by Night, In the Mood, Cinderella Man. Rarities & Few RFCD 1053.

1992 *Over the Europe*. Two-disc set: live performance (Europe, 1992) of Intro/Force Ten, Limelight, Freewill, Red Sector A, Time Stand Still, Dreamline, Bravado, Roll the Bones, Show Don't Tell, The Big Money, Ghost of a Chance, Subdivisions, The Pass, Where's My Thing?, The Rhythm Method, Closer to the Heart, Xanadu, Superconductor, Tom Sawyer, The Spirit of Radio, 2112 Overture, Finding My Way, La Villa Strangiato, Anthem, Red Barchetta, The Spirit of Radio (Reprise), Cygnus X-1. Metal Crash MECD 2084/2085.

1992[?] *Pensacola*. Two-disc set: live performance (Pensacola, Florida, February 25, 1992) of Force Ten, Limelight, Freewill, Distant Early Warning, Time Stand Still, Dreamline, Bravado, Roll the Bones, Show Don't Tell, The Big Money, Ghost of a Chance, Subdivisions, The Task, Where's My Thing?, Closer to the Heart, The Rhythm Method, Superconductor, Tom Sawyer. Goregon Music GM4.

1992 *Run from the Fans*. Live performance (U.S.A., 1992) of Force Ten, Limelight, Time Stand Still, Roll the Bones, Freewill, Distant Early Warning, Ghost of a Chance, Xanadu/Superconductor, Tom Sawyer. Kiss the Stone KTS094.

1992   *Rush.* Two-disc set: live performance (Holland, May 3, 1992) of Intro, Force Ten, Limelight, Freewill, Distant Early Warning, Time Stand Still, Dreamline, Bravado, Roll the Bones, Intro, Show Don't Tell, The Big Money, Ghost of a Chance, Subdivisions, The Pass, Where's My Thing?, Drum Solo, Closer to the Heart, Xanadu, Superconductor, Intro, Tom Sawyer, The Spirit of Radio, 2112, Finding My Way, La Villa Strangiato, Anthem, Red Barchetta, Cygnus X-1. Crystal Cat 301-2.

1992   *Rush 'N Roulette.* Two-disc set: live performance (U.S.A., 1992) of Force Ten, Limelight, Freewill, Distant Early Warning, Time Stand Still, Dream Life, Bravado, Roll the Bones, Show Don't Tell, Big Money, Ghost of a Chance, Subdivisions, The Pass, Where's My Thing?, Drum Solo, Closer to the Heart, Xanadu, Superconductor, Tom Sawyer, The Spirit of Radio, 2112, Finding My Way, La Villa Stragiato, Anthem. Silver Rarities SIRA 54/55.

1992   *The Story of Kings.* Live performance (U.S.A., 1992) of Force Ten, Limelight, Time Stand Still, Roll the Bones, Freewill, Distant Early Warning, Ghost of a Chance, Xanadu/Superconductor, Tom Sawyer, Bravado, Subdivisions, The Spirit of Radio, Anthem, Red Barchetta, The Spirit of Radio. Red Devil RED 004.

1993   *Counterparts.* Animate, Stick It Out, Cut to the Chase, Nobody's Hero, Between Sun & Moon, Alien Shore, The Speed of Love, Double Agent, Leave That Thing Alone, Cold Fire, Everyday Glory. Atlantic Anthem 82528 2.

1993   *Diamonds in the Waste.* Live performance (Mecca Arena, Milwaukee, March 24, 1986) of The Big Money, New World Man, Subdivisions, Manhattan Project, Middletown Dreams, Witch Hunt, Red Sector A, Marathon, Mystic Rhythms, Distant Early Warning, Territories. Blue Moon Records 1993 BMCD 007.

1993   *A Right to Passage.* Live performance (Pink Pop Festival, Geleen, Holland, June 4, 1979) of Passage to Bangkok, Xanadu, The Trees, Closer to the Heart, La Villa Strangiato, 2112, In the Mood, Something for Nothing. Rockdreams 92050.

1993   *Rush Hour, Greatest Hits Live.* Live performances (U.S.A, 1989, 1992) of The Spirit of Radio, Closer to the Heart, Limelight, Freewill, Distant Early Warning, Time Stand Still, Bravado, The Temples of Syrinx, Tom Sawyer, The Big Money, Ghost of a Chance, Subdivisions, The Pass, Where's My Thing?, Red Barchetta, The Spirit of Radio (Closing Section). Living Legend Records LLRCD 221.

1994   *Closer to Our Heart.* Live performance (Madison Square Garden, March 9, 1994) of Intro/Dreamline, The Spirit of Radio, The Analog Kid, Cold Fire, Time Stand Still, Nobody's Hero, Roll the Bones, Animate, Stick It Out, Double Agent, Limelight, Mystic Rhythms, Closer to the Heart, Show Don't Tell. Metal Crash MECD1160.

1994   *Come to a Standstill.* Two-disc set: live performance (Jacksonville, Florida, March 2, 1994) of Dreamline, The Spirit of Radio, The Analog Kid, Cold Fire, Time Stand Still, Nobody's Hero, Roll the Bones, Animate, Stick It Out, Double Agent, Limelight, Mystic Rhythms, Closer to the Heart, Show Don't Tell, Leave That Thing Alone, The Rhythm Method, The Trees, Xanadu, Tom Sawyer, Force Ten, YYZ, (and performed in Seattle, May 21, 1986) Manhattan Project, Middletown Dreams, Red Sector A, Marathon. Flashback 05. 94.0230.

1994   *Gangster of Boats.* Two-disc set: live performance (Uno Lakefront Arena, New Orleans, January 23, 1994) of Also Sprach Zarathustra, Dreamline, The Spirit of Radio, The Analog Kid, Cold Fire, Time Stand Still, Nobody's Hero, Roll the Bones, Animate, Stick It Out, Double Agent, Limelight, Mystic Rhythms, Closer to the Heart, Show Don't Tell, Leave That Thing Alone, The Rhythm Method, The Trees, Xanadu, Tom Sawyer, Force Ten, YYZ, (and performed at Cornhusk Arena, Omaha, Nebraska, April 2, 1988) Subdivisions, Marathon, Manhattan Project, Lock and Key, Mission. Insect Records IST 21/22.

1994   *Northern Heroes.* Two-disc set: live performance (Pensacola Civic Center, January 22, 1994) of Dreamline, The Spirit of Radio, The Analog Kid, Cold Fire, Time Stand Still, Nobody's Hero, Roll the Bones, Animate, Stick It Out, Double Agent, Limelight, Mystic Rhythms, Closer to the Heart, Show Don't Tell, Leave That Thing Alone, Drum Solo, The Trees, Xanadu/Prelude, Hemispheres, Tom Sawyer, Force Ten, YYZ. Cocomelos Records CM 025/26.

1994   *Red Barchetta.* Live performance (Montreal Forum, May, 1981) of Limelight, Tom Sawyer, The Trees, Xanadu, Red Barchetta, Freewill, Closer to the Heart, By-Tor and the Snow Dog, In the End, In the Mood. Live Storm LSCD 51055.

1994   *Storm in St. Petersburg.* Two-disc set: live performance (ThunderDome, St. Petersburg, Florida, March 4, 1994) of Dreamline, The Spirit of Radio, The Analog Kid, Cold Fire, Time Stand Still, Nobody's Hero, Roll the Bones, Animate, Stick It Out, Double Agent, Limelight, Mystic Rhythms, Closer to the Heart, Show Don't Tell, Leave That Thing Alone, Drum Solo, Medley: The Trees/Xanadu/Hemispheres/Tom Sawyer, Force Ten, YYZ (and listed as "Bonus Tracks, recorded elsewhere) Marathon, Red Barchetta, The Pass, War Paint, The Mission. Home Records HR5973/74.

A RUSH VIDEOGRAPHY

1985   *Through the Camera Eye.* Distant Early Warning, Vital Signs, The Body Electric, Afterimage, Subdivisions, Tom Sawyer, The Enemy Within, Countdown. PolyGram Music Video/RCA/Columbia Pictures 60466.

1986   *Grace Under Pressure Tour.* The Spirit of Radio, The Enemy Within, The Weapon, Witch Hunt, New World Man, Distant Early Warning, Red Sector A, Closer to the Heart, Medley: YYZ/Temples of Syrinx/Tom Sawyer, Medley: Vital Signs/Finding My Way/In the Mood, The Big Money. PolyGram Music Video/RCA/Columia Pictures 60607.

1987   *Exit...Stage Left.* Limelight, Tom Sawyer, The Trees, Instrumental, Xanadu, Red Barchetta, Freewill, Closer to the Heart, YYZ, Medley: By-Tor and the Snow Dog/In the End/In the Mood/2112 Finale, YYZ (instrumental). PolyGram Music Video/RCA/Columbia Pictures 60285.

1989   *A Show of Hands.* The Big Money, Marathon, Turn the Page, Prime Mover, Manhattan Project, Closer to the Heart, Red Sector A, Force Ten, Mission, Territories, The Rhythm Method/Drum Solo, The Spirit of Radio, Tom Sawyer, 2112/La Villa Strangiato/In the Mood. PolyGram Music Video 041 760-3.

1990   *Chronicles.* Closer to the Heart, The Trees, Limelight, Tom Sawyer, Red Barchetta, Subdivisions, Distant Early Warning, Red Sector A, The Big Money, Mystic Rhythms, Time Stand Still, Lock and Key. Anthem/Polygram Music Video 082 765-3.

SELECTED BIBLIOGRAPHY

Barrett, William. *Irrational Man: A Study in Existentialist Philosophy*. Garden City, NY: Doubleday Anchor Books, 1962.

Berger, Peter L., and Thomas Luckmann. *The Social Construction of Reality: A Treatise in the Sociology of Knowledge*. Garden City, NY: Doubleday Anchor Books, 1967.

Bergman, Ingmar. *Fanny and Alexander* (Translated by Alan Blair). New York: Pantheon Books, 1982.

Cox, Harvey. *The Feast of Fools: A Theological Essay on Festivity and Fantasy*. New York: Harper & Row, 1972.

Dostoyevsky, Fyodor. *The Brothers Karamazov* (Translated by Constance Garnett). New York: New American Library, 1957.

Goethe, Johann Wolfgang von. *Faust I and II* (Translated by Philip Wayne). Baltimore: Penguin Books, 1968, 1976.

Goffman, Erving. *The Presentation of Self in Everyday Life*. Garden City, NY: Doubleday Anchor Books, 1959.

Guthrie, W. K. C. *The Greek Philosophers, from Thales to Aristotle*. New York: Harper & Row, 1960.

Heidegger, Martin. *Being and Time* (Translated by John Macquarrie and Edward Robinson). New York: Harper & Row, 1962.

———. *What Is Called Thinking* (Translated by J. Glenn Gray). New York: Harper & Row, 1968.

Hesse, Hermann. *Siddhartha* (Translated by Hilda Rosner). New York: New Directions, 1951.

Hoffer, Eric. *The True Believer*. New York: Harper & Row, 1951.

Humphreys, Christmas. *Buddhism*. Baltimore: Penguin Books, 1972.

Huxley, Aldous. *Brave New World*. New York: Harper & Row, 1969.

Jaynes, Julian. *The Origin of Consciousness in the Breakdown of the Bicameral Mind*. Boston: Houghton Mifflin, 1977.

Jung, C. G. *The Undiscovered Self* (Translated by R. F. C. Hull). New York: New American Library, 1959.

Kaufmann, Walter. *The Faith of a Heretic*. Garden City, NY: Doubleday Anchor Books, 1963.

Kazantzakis, Nikos. *The Last Temptation of Christ*. New York: Bantam Books, 1968.

Kosinski, Jerzy. *Being There*. New York: Harcourt Brace Jovanovitch, 1971.

Lewis, C. S. *The Screwtape Letters; &, Screwtape Proposes a Toast*. New York: Macmillan Company, 1970.

Lovecraft, H. P. *The Tomb* and *Other Tales*. New York: Beagle Books, 1971.

———. *Fungi from Yuggoth and Other Poems*. New York: Ballantine Books, 1971.

Macquarrie, John. *Existentialism*. Baltimore: Penguin Books, 1978.

Marcus Aurelius. *Meditations* (Translated by Maxwell Staniforth). Baltimore: Penguin Books, 1976.

Miller, Calvin. *The Singer*. Downers Grove: InterVarsity Press, 1975.

Milton, John. *Paradise Lost and Other Poems*. New York: New American Library, 1961.

Nietzsche, Friedrich. *Thus Spake Zarathustra* (Translated by Walter Kaufmann). Baltimore: Penguin Books, 1978.

____. *Twilight of the Idols; The Anti-Christ* (Translated by R. J. Hollingdale). Baltimore: Penguin Books, 1990.

Orwell, George. *1984*. New York: New American Library, 1949.

Pieper, Josef. *Leisure, the Basis of Culture* (Translated by Alexander Dru). London: Faber and Faber, 1952.

Pirsig, Robert M. *Zen and the Art of Motorcycle Maintenance: An Inquiry into Values*. New York: Bantam Books, 1979.

Plato. *The Last Days of Socrates* (Translated by Hugh Tredennick). Baltimore: Penguin Books, 1970.

____. *Protagoras and Meno* (Translated by W. K. C. Guthrie). Baltimore: Penguin Books, 1977.

____. *The Republic* (Translated by Desmond Lee). Baltimore: Penguin Books, 1975.

____. *The Symposium* (Translated by Walter Hamilton). Baltimore: Penguin Books, 1978.

Postman, Neil, and Charles Weingartner. *Teaching as a Subversive Activity*. New York: Delacorte Press, 1969.

Rand, Ayn. *Anthem*. New York: New American Library, 1946.

____. *The Fountainhead*. New York: New American Library, 1943.

____. *Romantic Manifesto*. New York: New American Library, 1971.

____. *The Virtue of Selfishness: A New Concept of Egoism*. New York: New American Library, 1964.

Saunders, Jason L. (editor). *Greek and Roman Philosophy After Aristotle*. New York: The Free Press, Macmillan Company, 1966.

Skinner, B. F. *Beyond Freedom and Dignity*. New York: Bantam Books, 1972.

____. *Walden Two*. New York: Macmillan Company, 1962.

Tolkien, J. R. R. *The Hobbit*. Boston: Houghton Mifflin Co., 1966.

____. *The Lord of the Rings*. Boston: Houghton Mifflin Co., 1966.

Weales, Gerald Clifford (editor). *Arthur Miller: Death of a Salesman: Text and Criticism*. New York: Viking Press, 1967.

Weinbaum, Stanley G. *The New Adam*. New York: Avon Books, 1969.

Whitman, Walt. *Leaves of Grass*. New York: Thomas Y. Crowell Company, 1933.

Williams, Paul. *Mahayana Buddhism: The Doctrinal Foundations*. New York: Routledge, 1989.

Wilson, Colin. *The Laurel & Hardy Theory of Consciousness*. San Francisco: Robert Briggs Associates, 1986.

____. *The Outsider*. London: Pan Books, 1978.

____. *Religion and the Rebel*. Boston: Houghton Mifflin Co., 1957.

____. *The Strength to Dream*. London: Sphere Books, 1979.

INDEX

155

Printed in the United States
4938

9 781587 151026